think globally, act locally 97 D

UNDERSTANDING HUMAN RESOURCE MANAGEMENT

gramsi and face — 102 C

See 24D, 27-28, 28-29
  42A, 82A, 87, 90, 93, 97, 100, 102C,
                                      108-110, 122A-
KSA *knowledge, skills and*   129B,
        abilities

SHRM — *Strategic HRM*

RBV *Resource based view* —

HRRC *Human Resource Retention*
              Capacity 69 D

KCU *Knowledge Creation and*
        Utilization. 77 D

absorptive capacity of learning 83 D

making old knowledge relevant
                              84 C

KBV *Knowledge*

expatriate failure 98B

Globalisation defined 108 A
                            -110

MANAGING WORK AND ORGANIZATIONS SERIES

Edited by Dr Graeme Salaman, Professor of Organisation Studies in the Faculty of Social Sciences and the Open Business School, the Open University

Current titles:

Peter Anthony: *Managing Culture*
David Casey: *Managing Learning in Organizations*
Timothy Clark: *Managing Consultants*
Rohan Collier: *Combating Sexual Harassment in the Workplace*
Paul Iles: *Managing Staff Selection and Assessment*
Ken N. Kamoche: *Understanding Human Resource Management*
Ian McLoughlin and Stephen Gourlay: *Enterprise Without Unions*
Graeme Salaman: *Managing*
Jenny Shaw and Diane Perrons: *Making Gender Work*
Keith Sisson and John Storey: *The Realities of Human Resource Management*
John Storey and Keith Sisson: *Managing Human Resources and Industrial Relations*

UNDERSTANDING HUMAN RESOURCE MANAGEMENT

Ken N. Kamoche

"management" itself questioned 120c

Teamwork — 122B

Open University Press
Buckingham · Philadelphia

Open University Press
Celtic Court
22 Ballmoor
Buckingham
MK18 1XW

email: enquiries@openup.co.uk
world wide web: www.openup.co.uk

and
325 Chestnut Street
Philadelphia, PA 19106, USA

First Published 2001

A catalogue record of this book is available from the British Library

ISBN   0 335 20374 4 (hb)   0 335 20373 6 (pb)

Library of Congress Cataloging-in-Publication Data
Understanding human resource management/Ken N. Kamoche
    p.   cm. — (Managing work and organizations series)
    Includes bibliographical references and index.
    ISBN 0-335-20374-4   0 335 20373 6 pb
    1. Personnel management.   I. Kamoche, Ken N.   II. Series.
HF5549.U4164 2001
658.3–dc21

                                                        00-060651

Typeset by Type Study, Scarborough
Printed in Great Britain by St Edmundsbury Press Ltd,
Bury St Edmunds, Suffolk

Dedicated to all my family in Kenya and elsewhere

CONTENTS

ACKNOWLEDGEMENTS

This book has benefited from numerous discussions I have had over the years with many friends and colleagues, managers and policy makers around the world. My heartfelt thanks go to all of you. Many of these ideas have also endured lively classroom discussions in places like Birmingham, Lisbon, Bangkok, Hong Kong and Darwin where I have been fortunate to teach. I am particularly indebted to Graeme Salaman who felt there was space in the highly robust HRM debate for a book such as this one, and for his very helpful suggestions. I would also like to thank Sam Aryee for his detailed comments on an earlier draft, and Randall Schuler and Karen Legge for their comments and support. Finally I would like to thank John Skelton and the Open University Press staff for their help. Any errors or omissions remain my own.

1

INTRODUCTION

This book is the culmination of about ten years of enquiry into the meaning and nature of human resource management (HRM). During that time, the field has undergone a substantial transformation, one which began a lot earlier and which is not likely to end soon. In that regard, it is probably fair to say that HRM is in a constant state of flux. The discipline concerned with the management of people, the employer–employee relationship or labour regulation has of course been around for as long as there have been formal organizations. Whether they called it personnel management, personnel administration or strategic human resource management is immaterial. The important question is what actually goes on in this process, what sets of policies and practices constitute the managers' chosen approach and what are the key assumptions underlying these managerial choices.

An overriding assumption in the literature is that the purpose of HRM is to help organizations achieve their objectives, which are essentially seen in terms of performance. According to Brewster (1999), 'the value of this paradigm lies in the simplicity of focus, the coalescing of the research around this shared objective and the clear relationship with the demands of industry'. Conversely it ignores the other relevant stakeholders. All too often we see books on HRM that merely concern themselves with questions like 'How can we manage better?' 'What practices are appropriate for what organizations?' 'How can we best adopt these practices to meet organizational objectives?' Such approaches are usually devoid of theory, are manifestly functionalist in their stated purpose to serve organizational ends while ignoring other stakeholders, and are clearly underpinned by a rationalist epistemology which works on the basis that the reality around us is knowable, and accessible through systematic analysis. The role of the academic in helping organizations achieve their 'strategic objectives' through HRM is not necessarily disputed here. However, such efforts must not lose sight of a fundamental tenet of good scholarship: to understand as fully as possible the nature of the phenomenon – HRM – its social, political, ethical and cultural dimensions, rather than merely how to make it work better.

The rationalist epistemology leads to the conclusion that through rigorous systematic analysis of the reality around us we can reach the truth, which consists of universal knowledge. This eventually leads both researchers and managers alike to adopt or recommend 'solutions' which have been found to work elsewhere. While few people today are prepared to ignore such contingencies as culture, size, organizational form and so forth, there is still an expectation that so long as we allow for such minor inconveniences, human resource management *can* be made to work. HRM thus becomes at once a set of practices for realizing managerially defined business outcomes and a mirror of the desired reality which is then projected onto the organization. There is, however, more to human resource management than this scenario would suggest. What constitutes HRM, how it is constituted, for whom it is constituted and by whom it is applied are issues that are just as problematic as the issue of what sorts of organizations we are designing to achieve these ends.

As human resource management metamorphosed into *strategic human resource management*, it became *de rigueur* to treat it as a *source of competitive advantage*. A vast amount of literature supporting or trying to support this contention has emerged since the mid-1980s. It is more or less taken for granted that there is something out there called *competitive advantage* which it is in the firm's interest to achieve. It is so much in vogue that many writers never bother to define exactly what they mean by this; they simply claim

2

Technique driven.

that by doing such and such, by adopting such and such an HR practice, the organization can achieve competitive advantage. Maybe there is no need to reinvent the wheel with every publication but it would certainly help if we had better clarification as to what exactly the superior practices are supposed to achieve. This issue is tackled in Chapter 3.

There appears to be a fallacy in recommending practices with universal appeal and supposed universal application. If all the firms are doing the same thing, implementing the same sets of HRM or any other practices, then it becomes difficult to see how each of them can gain an edge over all the rest if competitive advantage is about the capacity to outperform rivals. This trend is in part due to a commonly taken-for-granted assumption that the tacit purpose of scholarship in the field of management is to improve organizational performance, a contender for competitive advantage.

This is not to deny the existence of the corpus of knowledge which both queries this assumption and devotes itself to the critical analysis of the unspoken and sometimes explicit purposes and interests of the stakeholders who are seeking 'competitive advantage'. The volume of critical analyses into the nature, meaning and intents of the proponents of HRM is miniscule when compared to the vast literature which is committed to advancing the interests of organizations by discovering how they can better achieve their objectives. This basically means that we are likely to end up knowing more and more about the methods and practices that apparently work, and less and less about why such methods and practices have been devised in the first place. If we are not clear as to the origins and political purposes of these practices, we will equally be at a loss as to why they do not work quite as well as expected when circumstances change.

Three such circumstances are the complexities of the international context, technological advancement and the uncertainties of the future. The effects of globalization are being felt all around the world today. The opening up of foreign markets, trade liberalization, and developments in new technologies including the onset of e-commerce are changing the way businesses operate. This is in turn having a profound effect on the way people are managed. The old models of internationalization are no longer reflected in reality. One such model holds that the firm begins with 'domestic' operations, then it opens a foreign sales subsidiary, followed by an international division. Such a firm goes through stages: domestic, international, global and transnational. Each of these stages requires some specific sets of practices in the way people are managed, and the kinds of 'international skills' and competencies they require.

Geographical location and orientation play a key role in the linear models, which means that in the initial stages when the firm is still essentially domestic, knowledge of international business practices and possession of international skills is minimal. All this is changing rapidly. A firm can set up its business on the internet and begin trading globally from day one. There are no stages of internationalization and no specific transition between domestic and global. An international orientation and an appreciation of business practices and cultures are inevitable and must be built up in a relatively short time-frame. International skills must be developed right from the outset. Currently not all organizations have the flexibility to adapt themselves to these new technological opportunities, but it is just a matter of time before the entire paradigm of doing business and managing across borders undergoes a complete revamp. We consider these issues in more detail in Chapters 2, 7 and 9.

The foregoing of course has implications for the way we understand or misunderstand HRM. Failure to anticipate the trends and act accordingly will mean organizations run the risk of utilizing their stock of human resources inappropriately at best. At worst, it means misusing and mismanaging resources. This of course depends on how much value managers attach to human resources and what they understand by human resources in the first place. If people are seen as the repository of organizational knowledge, it would make sense for managers to attach a high value to such a valuable resource, which means that people will be treated as a potential source of added value. Put simply, the judicious use of their skills will generate profits. As such, we can expect mechanisms will be put in place to ensure that these people will be treated well in terms of providing them with opportunities for personal growth, attractive rewards, and a chance to cultivate their creativity. We would also expect the organization to institute retention mechanisms to ensure that this valuable resource does not walk away.

On the other hand, where people are only treated as sources of profit and little else, which means they are easily dispensed with when no longer needed, we are likely to end up with a transactional climate in which each party is driven by its own self-interest. People will thus be seen as just another input into the production process with nothing else that warrants additional efforts to retain them. People in turn will treat organizations merely as a source of immediate benefits, financial or otherwise. In reality the retention of people proceeds on a selective basis. We see this happening in this age of downsizing and corporate restructuring. These questions are considered in Chapters 3 to 6.

Understanding the dynamics of HRM also means coming to terms with some uncomfortable truths: that business strategies appear to have a life of their own, or at least one propelled by an uncompromising imperative for organizational survival which is generally unforgiving of inefficiency and waste. Therefore, even though people are often defined as the most important asset, they also seem to be one of the most expendable when the very survival of a business organization is at stake, thought to be at stake, or when managers come under pressure to manage costs. This has resulted in a paradox in which managers' claims about the importance of the 'greatest asset' are not borne out in reality (Drucker, 1992). In fact, in an analysis of intangible assets, Hall (1993) found that the most valuable were company and product reputation and employee knowhow, in that order.

Recent research on the 'psychological contract', for example by Rousseau and her colleagues, has been shedding new light on the complexity of the employer–employee relationship (see for example Robinson *et al.*, 1994; Robinson and Rousseau, 1994). These authors have argued, inter alia, that one party's perceived contribution obligates the other to reciprocate. From the foregoing, the question that arises is how prevalent and sustainable this notion of perceived *reciprocity* is today. This appears to be a blind spot in employment relationships which are more concerned with the tangibility of what the parties are able to secure from each other. On a more optimistic note, Burack (1993) proposes a new basis for a psychological contract which includes elements like 'good faith' in maintaining employment continuity and a 'family' metaphor in which 'managers treat people with respect and provide real support in new paradigm organizations' (p. 159). We explore these and related concepts in Chapter 8.

Mechanisms such as performance appraisal give managers the opportunity to make supposedly rational choices as to the relative value of the contributions of the employees. These imputed values in turn serve as a surrogate for the value the appraisers place on the employees themselves. Whether the mechanisms are in effect rational or not is immaterial here; the important point is that tools are available and can be invented, if need be, to differentiate between people *vis-à-vis* the organizational requirements and imperative for growth. This argument parallels Davis and Moore's (1966) functional theory of stratification in which society decides who gets what positions based on the perceived functional importance of their talents and training. The perceived importance of people's skills either as individuals or *vis-à-vis* other competing resources plays a role (alongside other factors including favouritism and bias) in determining what positions they take in the organization and whether they retain these positions in times of organizational turbulence. This raises an issue that is not often recognized in HRM debates – the perceptions that people have about their own 'value'. This is attributable to the practice of analysing HRM from an organizational perspective. Do people think of themselves as a valuable resource? Do they think of themselves as the most important asset? What are their expectations in the information age and are their voices being heard? There seems to be a need for more research from this perspective and to reconcile it to the predominant organizational/ managerial one. I attempt to explore these issues in Chapter 3.

This book therefore is about what it means to manage people, and how this is changing and is likely to change as we advance into an increasingly complex world where many of our assumptions about management are constantly being challenged. Various authors have attempted to explain human resource management in different ways, and the critical–analytical literature continues to bring us closer to gaining a more complete picture of what HRM really is about. Schuler and Jackson (1999) have recently suggested the use of a variety of theoretical frameworks, including *qu. is there a recogn. dynamic betw indiv and corporate - as in voluntary self-sacrific for the good of all.*

institutional theory, resource dependence theory, human capital theory and so forth. Theoretical frameworks are useful analytical devices whose contribution to unravelling the HRM phenomenon is evident in the robust literature. Our arguments here are not framed in an overarching theoretical framework; in fact, one key objective is to examine the value of some of the more recent frameworks, such as the resource-based view (see Chapter 4).

Questions about the use and legitimacy of control, using skills and competencies to enhance organizational performance, eliciting commitment and fostering a viable organizational climate and so forth have been debated for some time now. Similarly, managers, academics and consultants have covered the 'practices' terrain very thoroughly – what selection, training and performance appraisal techniques are being used where and how. Others have addressed what constitutes HRM in 'reality' *vis-à-vis* the claims made about it, how it differs from other mechanisms for managing people, and so forth. The debate has been shifting to other areas of theoretical sophistication, building bridges with disciplines like strategic management, international management, critical theory, post-modernism and so forth. These developments point to the different ways in which researchers define and approach their problematics, how this is underpinned by certain assumptions within their respective paradigms, and what they see as their role in these processes.

These themes, assumptions and theoretical perspectives have a profound bearing on the questions this book addresses. In fact, the discussion goes further and questions whether the current academic undertakings have succeeded in giving us a complete picture of the dynamics of managing people. This is a difficult question because it involves questioning the whole idea of 'managing', and trying to discover whether the phenomenon of HRM should actually be seen as something other than 'managing'. I consider this question in Chapter 8.

The foregoing is a general introduction to the challenges I have embraced in this book. Below, I offer a more specific summary of each of the subsequent chapters. Chapter 2 begins by examining the role of organizations in managing people, by focusing on the notion of improving the human condition. It locates the discussion in a historical context and looks at the potential future directions in the enduring task of 'humanizing work'. The chapter goes on to consider some of the definitive themes in the current conceptions of HRM, and concludes by querying whether we are now coming to a mature phase of HRM.

Chapter 3 considers the emergent version of HRM: strategic HRM. This chapter tackles some controversial issues in the strategic HRM debate, such as the idea that the utilization of human resources can be a source of competitive advantage. This argument appears to be part of a bandwagon effect that began in the mid-1980s and evolved mainly at the conceptual level before researchers moved ahead with empirical investigations which have also raised a new set of concerns. The chapter discusses the practical implications of these academic debates with regard to questions like training and retention. It also proposes further research from the point of view of those most affected by the actions arising from these developments.

Chapter 4 takes the strategic HRM debate further by examining a major contribution of the 1990s: the resource-based view (RBV). Although the concept itself emerged much earlier in strategic management, its 'discovery' by human resource theorists is a more recent phenomenon. The resource-based view refocuses attention on the resources that exist within the organization and over which the organization has some control. The discussion traces the development of this concept and its implications for the management of people. This discussion also identifies some weaknesses in the application of the RBV to a discipline as complex as HRM. It also challenges the dominance of the external environment paradigm and the enduring emphasis on practices at the expense of resources.

Chapter 5 tackles one dimension of the resource-based view that has only received limited attention in the HRM literature so far: appropriation. Within the strategic management debate, appropriation is understood to be the firm's ability to retain for its own use the benefits of utilizing resources under its control. The firm's appropriative arms logically stretch into the HRM domain to the extent that managers are utilizing human *resources* for specific organizational ends. Herein lies the paradox: the forms of control normally applied for other resources are likely to be of limited use in the case of human resources which organizations do not, strictly speaking own. This leads us to a consideration of the limits of appropriation, the importance of employee retention in the appropriation regime, and the use of resource and mobility barriers.

Chapter 6 takes a critical look at the concept of knowledge. 'Knowledge' has become the latest buzzword in organization science as well as in the world of business. The discussion brings together some of the earlier constitutive strands in the conception of knowledge, from information management and the power of experts to questions about the production of knowledge. The chapter then offers a number of perspectives to elucidate the concept of knowledge, including its social construction, and the extent to which it is self-perpetuating and context-specific. The concept of knowledge gives us a fresh approach into the human resource management debate, in particular the challenges of managing the tacit dimension, and the challenge of securing organizational control over it. This chapter also explores the interface between knowledge management and the resource-based view.

Chapter 7 aims to locate the HRM debate within the international context. That is not to say that the previous chapters concern themselves with 'domestic' issues; rather, this chapter identifies the key issues that come to the surface when operations take on a decidedly international complexion. This chapter takes issue with the somewhat narrow perspectives that have characterized international HRM so far, such as the preoccupation with serving the needs of multinational firms, the adjustment problems of expatriates and cross-cultural management. The global arena is a lot more complex than that. It requires a concerted effort to understand the socio-political and economic circumstances of those affected by global business and trade. The issue of 'globalization' has recently been getting a lot of bad press. This chapter identifies some of its effects on HRM, particularly in the special case of developing countries, and the challenge of appropriation in an international context.

Chapter 8 raises some additional issues about the context of business, suggesting that the social context has a lot more to offer to our understanding of the challenges of managing than is readily evident. It examines the suitability of mechanisms like the 'community concept' and the idea of 'facilitating resourcefulness' as a way of understanding the task of 'managing'.

The final chapter wraps up the discussion by suggesting some ways in which we might begin to think of human resource management in an increasingly turbulent world. It also offers some suggestions as to how the debates covered in this book might encourage further research.

THE HRM DEBATE: A REAPPRAISAL

As we enter the new millennium, the time appears opportune to re-examine the extent to which modern organizations have contributed – or failed to contribute – to improving the human condition. The industrial and technological age we live in today has changed dramatically in the last hundred and indeed thousand years, and at the current pace of technological advancement we can expect that in the next hundred and thousand years the world will have changed beyond our wildest dreams. So will organizations and the roles of those who manage and work for them.

Formal organizations played a fundamental role in shaping our lives in the last century; one can only speculate as to how this role will change. One thing we can be sure of is that turbulence and uncertainty will continue to be dominant themes in the industrial and competitive arenas, and that this will necessarily have far-reaching consequences for the organization of work, and the management of people. This suggests the need to question the relevance and suitability of extant forms of *organizing* and a re-appraisal of their effectiveness *vis-à-vis* the unpredictable realities that are likely to unfold in the new millennium. In particular for the purposes of this book, we are concerned with those forms of organizing that pertain to people management, labour regulation and organizational control.

Exactly a hundred years ago, the field of management was taking brave, albeit tentative steps into scholarly debate in the form of 'industrial betterment', the recipe of welfare improvement programmes that were being popularized by a selection of enlightened American corporations (e.g. Olmstead, 1900; Tolman, 1900). These practices constituted a new realization that industrialists should actively seek to improve the conditions of the working classes through the revolutionary principles of cooperation and partnerships and by introducing forms of profit-sharing, social-welfare, academic and sanitation facilities (see also Barley and Kunda, 1992).

These ideas were being implemented almost a hundred years after they were first promulgated by visionary social reformers like Robert Owen (1813). This 'enlightenment' was largely a western phenomenon, a point that must now be recognized in view of the fact that much of what today constitutes 'modern management' draws heavily from a western social–economic and psychological tradition, yet the full implications of this are only now beginning to be addressed in emergent disciplines like 'cross-cultural management'.

While social reformers in America and Europe were making their daring forays into the workplace, other regions like much of Africa and Asia were in the throes of colonialism or foreign occupation where foreign industrialists subjected local workers to conditions that would have been unthinkable in the west. It was not surprising, therefore, that independence struggles particularly in Africa inevitably fused industrial and economic with political objectives. Achieving political self-determination was perceived as entirely consistent with humanizing work and working conditions. This short historical perspective shows that the social and intellectual roots of many of the so-called enlightened human resource practices that rose to prominence in the last two decades in fact go back at least two hundred years.

This raises a number of issues: first, the time lag between the development or promulgation of apparently revolutionary concepts and their maturity into workable management practices. Clearly, resistance from powerful stakeholders (in this case industrialists) on both sides of the Atlantic hampered the development of these ideas, which they saw as an impediment to industrial growth and profitability. Paradoxically, it is alternative sets of industrialists who subsequently champion the visionary ideals and translate them into 'betterment programmes'. These initial efforts were underpinned by a strong moralist and religious ethos, as in the case of the Quaker movement or the founders of the Young Men's Christian Associations (YMCA). These efforts also reflected a strong Protestant work ethic, including the duty to work and assume responsibility for one's actions and destiny. Surprisingly, the role of religious, spiritual and moral values in organizational theory and practice has been little studied so far.

A second question relates to the effectiveness of these measures in resolving the human concerns they purport to address. Industrial betterment has manifested itself in different guises over the years, from the earliest forms noted above and the use of 'welfare officers' who were to metamorphose later into personnel officers and latterly into human resource managers, to the current concern with issues like gain sharing, employee assistance programmes, empowerment, teamwork, mentoring and so forth. What have these measures really achieved for those at whom they are targeted? The evidence is patchy and inconclusive, and we may never know what the complete picture looks like.

Part of the difficulty lies in the non-measurability of these initiatives, which may perhaps lead some to disregard the initiatives altogether as wishy-washy. On the other hand, there is a danger in taking on practices in order to be seen to be caring, or simply because the practice is 'flavour of the month'. This is most evident in the hype that often surrounds the 'discovery' of a new-fangled management practice, including, some would argue, the adoption of the name (and perhaps the practice of) 'human resource management' itself in place of 'personnel management'.

A third question is: what is the next stage in this apparent trajectory in 'humanizing' work? The moralistic and do-gooding themes in industrial betterment were for a while eclipsed by the more rationalistic approach to re-engineering work systematically via Taylorism and 'scientific management'. Following the then well-established tradition of many influential mechanical engineers before him, Frederick Taylor devised mechanisms for improving factory productivity and efficiency through the enhancement of predictability and control and by reducing the scope for human intervention, error and waste. This new thinking held a strong appeal to managers who saw embedded in it a rational logic that resonated with their search for efficiency. It is for this reason that Tayloristic ideals have had a lasting legacy in management.

The failure of scientific management to deliver the promised efficient industrial society ultimately led to a re-emergence of the industrial–social betterment ethos in the form of the 'human relations movement'. Without rehearsing the sequence of events that has seen one school of thought superseded by another in the course of the last century, it is worth noting that two key themes have survived more or less in tandem during that period with varying degrees of prominence: the concern for performance (individual and organizational) and the concern with the 'human side of enterprise' (including 'welfare' issues).

These twin themes have been tied together by an inherent tension that perpetually places managers in an apparently irreconcilable dilemma. In the new millennium, this tension is not likely to go away easily. Advances in technology have redefined this tension and will continue to do so, but it is not clear whether a viable compromise can be realized. The socio-technical school of thought was one of the earlier efforts to confront this question head-on. In a series of investigations into the effects of technological change, the notion was put forward of a working group as an interdependent socio-technical system, as opposed to merely being one or the other (e.g. Emery and Trist, 1960). This inherent mutual interaction was deemed to generate economic validity in the sense that joint optimization would result in the realization of desirable psychological and performative outcomes.

The debate has since evolved in a number of different directions, which have contributed profoundly to unravelling the mystery of the people–technology interface. Many issues, however, remain unresolved, and will continue to exercise the best minds for years to come. One issue is that of the increasing complexity of technology as typified by the Internet explosion and all it promises in terms of telecommunications, information flow, e-commerce and so forth. The technological revolution at the turn of the twentieth century in many ways resembles *but* transcends the industrial revolution that preceded it two hundred years ago.

Human Resource Manipulation?

Or is this objection a symptom of individualism?

should managers be accountable?

Environments (internal and external) are themselves changing at an unprecedented rate, raising new challenges about appropriate methods of production, organizational structure and design, and how to manage the environmental turbulence in order to achieve performance/productivity objectives.

The quest for such objectives must be located firmly within the organizational social–political context, which points to the tension noted above. What organizations (as expressed by management) want in terms of strategic objectives and performance standards may only partially converge with what the employees themselves want. Reconciling the needs of both in order to ensure the uninterrupted flow of the production process has been a long-standing objective of management. The advent of technology has created opportunities for these sets of needs to be achieved in tandem.

Similarly it has also opened up a vast opportunity for the manifestation of divergence which, some would argue, is inevitable as the respective parties are committed to inherently divergent interests. In his assessment of personnel management, Watson (1986) argues that the employment relationship is not one of equal stakeholders but one in which the employer generally has more power. Therefore, even where welfare issues and family-friendly policies are considered, it is only to the extent that they meet the interests of the major stakeholders, and always at the least cost. Human resource management as commonly understood today remains wedded to this rationale. These concerns have given the unitarist–pluralist debate an entirely new complexion. These and related issues are explored in more detail in Chapters 3, 4 and 5.

The people–technology interface is just one aspect of the managerial challenge. Some of the most immediate effects of the technological revolution on people include a radical shift in work organization including changes in forms of networking and teamwork, widespread downsizing and 're-engineering', and a shift towards knowledge management. This latter topic is explored further in Chapter 6. The nature of work itself is going through a dramatic transformation, ranging from the initial mechanization and computerization of routines and the gradual replacement of human with technologically codified procedures to changes in what people actually do, when and how. This has necessitated a reassessment of the individual capabilities to respond to this technological challenge, in particular training for competence creation and the enhancement of the capacity to learn on a continuous basis. Below we consider some forces that have been responsible for the shaping of HRM as understood today.

Some notable definitive subthemes in the HRM debate

This section considers some of the subthemes that have shaped the evolution of the discipline concerned with the management of people. Many factors have contributed to the emergence of HRM and, no doubt, the phenomenon will continue to evolve in new directions as time goes by. The few subthemes discussed here are the ones which appear to have played a distinctly definitive role as typified in the literature. Our purpose here is not to rehearse these familiar subthemes but to re-examine them from a critical perspective, and determine how, when brought together, they enhance our overall understanding of HRM. By looking back critically at what has gone on before we might be better equipped to anticipate future developments. No chronological sequence is intended or implied.

The discovery of strategy

One of the most hotly debated issues in the 1980s and early 1990s was whether HRM was different from personnel management. There was a lot of concern to determine whether HRM offered anything new or whether, as some suspected, it was merely old wine in new bottles. Part of the debate was no doubt triggered by curiosity about whether HRM constituted a threat or an opportunity to personnel practitioners. Views about this are numerous and range from the cynical and dismissive to the near-evangelical. Skinner (1981) describes it as good intentions and whistling in the dark or averting unionization; for Armstrong (1987) it is 'the Emperor's new clothes' – suggesting the perpetuation of a falsehood. In a similar vein, Keenoy (1990) likened HRM to a wolf in sheep's clothing, an attempt to depict the hidden hand of control and managerial prerogative in the guise of 'commitment' and 'integrative practices'.

Some of these arguments reflected the scepticism that prevailed in the emergent phase of contemporary HRM. It is fair to say that the HRM debate has advanced beyond these initial concerns. The literature is replete with accounts of successful HRM initiatives in change management, training, performance management and so forth. How managers achieve organizational objectives through these initiatives may be viewed from two angles: people may be treated as just another factor of production; alternatively, they may be viewed as valued assets. Hence the 'hard' and 'soft' models of HRM (e.g. Legge, 1989, 1995; Storey, 1989). According to Legge (1989, 1995), the tensions inherent in this dichotomy lie at the heart of the nature of capitalism itself.

The debate still rages on about the motives underlying these initiatives, and whose interests they serve. Doubt still remains about the extent to which HRM fulfils a *strategic* function. This issue is pursued further in Chapter 3. It appears that the quest for a strategic dimension marked a watershed in the transformation of the personnel discipline and in its eventual conversion into (strategic) HRM. Whether this was fuelled by the personnel practitioners' (and researchers') quest for status or a desire to impact positively and *proactively* on managerial decision making, or whether it was indeed a genuine acknowledgement of the potential value of 'human capital', there is still a lot of controversy about the real value of HRM initiatives.

Many researchers see this value largely in terms of the extent to which HRM impacts on organizational performance. The more cynical observers would argue that in the process of achieving this performance, the realization of a real change for employees (over and above contractual arrangements) is not the explicit objective of many managers but may be treated as a desirable by-product. This can be attributed to the hard–soft dichotomy. Alternatively, it could be argued that the claim often made that people are the most important asset is not only revealed to be an exaggeration, but may not even be realistic from the point of view of managers grappling with elusive financial targets, loss of market share, demanding customers, pressure to contain costs, the threat of hostile takeovers and so forth. Of course people *are* important; it

17

would be ethically untenable, if not politically incorrect, to claim otherwise. However, although few managers would wish to be quoted as contradicting the 'people are our most valuable asset' refrain, the reality suggests otherwise.

The global recession of the 1980s and the financial crisis that began in Asia in 1997 have revealed the dispensability of people when difficult business decisions have to be made. We have gone through, and continue to witness, an era of downsizing, retrenchment, high unemployment globally, diminishing training budgets, 'flexible working' and short-term contracts, leading to widespread job insecurity. These have been some of the real effects of strategic business decisions, which for our purposes here also means that they reflect a substantial part of what it means to manage people 'strategically'. As such, these human resource decisions can be rationalized as being in the strategic interests of the organization. In the process, it is assumed that the interests of the employees being subjected to strategic decisions are somehow subsumed within those of the main stakeholders, which is debatable.

While in welfare states retrenched workers have access to welfare benefits, retraining opportunities and outplacement facilities, in poor countries retrenchment often means extreme poverty for an extended family that relies on a sole breadwinner. Business organizations are not, generally speaking, driven by a charitable concern for human needs, so we can expect to see them making decisions based on a putative rational assessment of the most efficient utilization of available assets to generate 'added value'. As Kamoche and Mueller (1998: 1035) have argued, the question of utilizing resources to generate and retain this added value needs to be addressed more explicitly in HRM. The incorporation of a 'strategic' dimension into HRM has not adequately demonstrated that this is possible. Will the new millennium bring about a new awareness of the sanctity of 'human resources' that does not preclude the generation of added value?

Change management

A substantial impetus for the popularization of HRM was provided by the drive to institute 'change management'. Organizations go through change all the time, and the last fifteen years have witnessed high degrees of turbulence and uncertainty that have forced people to consider change a permanent feature of their working lives. The change we are referring to here consists of the management-led but mostly market-inspired initiatives to introduce new technology, transform working practices, turn organizations round, realize successful mergers, acquisitions and strategic alliances, and so forth. The role of HRM in these efforts has increasingly been recognized as critical. Total quality management (TQM) for example initially focused on achieving transformative change at the micro-level in so-called quality circles whose agenda evolved around quality and productivity issues. As the scope of TQM expanded, the distinction between TQM and HRM gradually became blurred to the extent that many of the tenets of TQM have now been fully absorbed into mainstream HRM. Hardly anyone talks about TQM any more, except in so far as it relates to specific initiatives that are understood to fall under the rubric of HRM, including realizing production and quality improvements through skill utilization.

Technology-related change has had some of the most radical effects on the nature of work and the reorganization of working practices from the boardroom to the factory floor. These changes have in effect been a double-edged sword from the point of view of people who have been at once victims and beneficiaries, as computerization and automation gradually replaced human skills, leading to job loss, and simultaneously opened up opportunities for skill enhancement and self-improvement. Business Process Reengineering (BPR) was lauded as a refreshing new basis for modernization in the 1990s, with its goal of systematic redesign and revamping of entire organizational processes and structures. This post-Tayloristic phenomenon in effect aspired to minimize the role and presence of the human dimension, as witnessed through the concomitant downsizing.

The trend toward 'globalization' has also been reshaping the competitive landscapes and imposing new demands on people's adaptability to organizational change. Multinational organizations can now tap into far-flung markets and in the process instigate a homogenization of customer tastes through the marketing of 'global brands'. The pervasiveness of names like Coke, Nike

and McDonald's is testimony to the power of globalization. The power of the media has been instrumental in realizing this global trend; an equally important role has been played by strategic alliances, mergers and acquisitions that span continents and direct foreign investment by multinational companies into new territories that offer new opportunities for growth, relatively low labour costs, tax incentives, managerial expertise and so forth.

This expansionism has been associated with technology transfer, the introduction of new working practices including the reorganization of industrial relations as in the case of Japanese investments, and radical changes in national cultures. Diminishing domestic markets and intensifying competition have forced many organizations to seek greener pastures and new opportunities overseas. In a book that captured the mood of the global wave in the 1980s, Bartlett and Ghoshal (1989) assessed the forces of globalization and the ways in which multinational firms have embraced or failed to embrace the demands of global competition in the way they configure their competitive capabilities.

The external environment has been seen as the principal source of organizational change. For example, Child (1987) suggests that external competitive pressures result in the following types of strategic responses: demand risk – fluctuations in demand following intensified global competition lead to heightened flexibility and the need to improve quality; innovation risk – organizations are forced to improve their capacity to innovate after falling behind their competitors; risk of inefficiency – failure to match rivals' costs forces firms to undertake cost-reduction measures. These scenarios have important implications for HRM – the situational–contingent argument that HR responses will differ based on the extant organizational challenges.

This argument is at the heart of the rationale typically offered for strategic HRM, i.e. that HR decisions and strategies should flow from business/competitive decisions/strategies. The kinds of pressures that have prompted the global trend have had far-reaching effects on human resource strategies and practices. Attention has grown from a narrow concern with staffing policies for foreign subsidiaries to an awareness, at least on the part of some of the progressive multinational firms, of the importance of designing appropriate mechanisms for leveraging learning and disseminating knowledge across the organization. We discuss these issues in Chapter 6.

Culture and the search for excellence

Organizational culture has been discussed almost *ad nauseam*, and it is not my intention to tire the reader with another detailed discussion. My purpose here is to weave together a few strands that appear to shed some light on the generative forces behind the emergence of HRM as commonly understood. Interest in culture is a picture of constant transformation. From the earlier concerns with the constitutive elements of culture (norms, attitudes, values and beliefs) to the manifestations and creation of 'strong cultures' (Ouchi, 1981; Deal and Kennedy, 1982), attention shifted to the transformative effects of culture. The roots of some of the subsequent debates can be found in the seminal volume by Kilmann *et al.* (1985) which set out an agenda for research on corporate culture. The corporate culture phenomenon was welcomed enthusiastically by a large proportion of the academic community. Consultants and managers have also played a key role in preaching a gospel which many still consider a generic panacea to organizational ills.

It soon became clear to researchers that the legitimacy and practicality of the new fad could only be sustained if the debate went beyond the nebulous artefacts of culture like norms, values and attitudes to embrace specific human resource practices. Corporate culture was thus woven into employee selection, reward management and training (culminating eventually in cross-cultural training for international assignments). It is now recognized that the success of initiatives such as the introduction of new technology, instilling innovativeness and even having successful mergers largely depend on the cultivation of a supportive culture. Mergers and acquisitions are a particularly interesting case of the pivotal role of culture. Traditionally, managers and analysts tend to account for the expected synergy from such decisions in purely financial terms. When mergers subsequently come to grief, all manner of economic and financial explanations are invariably put forward.

There is now a creeping awareness that those less conspicuous

21

sets of assumptions that underpin behaviour and define how 'we do things around here' have a lot to answer for in such failed ventures. Culture is about people, how they relate to each other and to the structures that define their working environment, and it becomes imperative therefore that if these structures are to serve their intended organizational purpose the human resource question has to be brought to the fore. Managing the cultural aspects within the framework of HRM then becomes a matter of addressing attitudinal, behavioural and symbolic norms which are ultimately expected to yield performance outcomes. In short, having the right culture – one which takes account of people's needs – will ultimately impact on the 'bottom line', or so the argument goes. Kilmann *et al.* (1985: 429) conclude their extensive discussion with the view that 'recognizing the human need to understand and make sense of changing circumstances is a central part of managing the deepest levels of corporate culture'.

The excellence literature as epitomized by Peters and Waterman (1982) claims there are some generic approaches to managing which are likely to lead to organizational success. The literature offers fairly simplistic formulas which have neither been researched nor rigorously analysed, but are based on some isolated observations of 'successful' companies. To be fair, the 'excellence movement' has offered some interesting lessons – it has refocused attention on culture and 'soft HRM', and in particular the critical issue of changing attitudes, formulating strong values and constantly generating an innovative spirit, rather than merely relying on managing by manipulating structures and systems. But excellence is a nebulous and indeterminate notion that is best left to the acritical and atheoretical evangelizing by management gurus.

In spite of the fact that most observers appear to take a functionalist view of the positive benefits of cultivating and inculcating 'strong' cultures, culture has a dark side to it. The negative and sometimes debilitating aspects of corporate culture have been recognized from time to time. For example, Kunda (1992) has explored the ideological problems associated with the excessive inculcation of supposedly integrative cultural values in a high-tech firm. The inculcation of culture can quickly turn into indoctrination which robs the individuals of any sense of identity outside their attachment to the organization and its values in which they must demonstrate an unquestioning acquiescence.

Indoctrination clearly raises an important ethical issue and is at odds with the concern for the 'softer' side of organization which includes human needs. Anthony (1994) writes that subordination to cultural authority and the methods cultural control imposes are likely to suppress values like openness, empowerment, risk taking and responsibility. The excellence movement has played a role in creating an 'enterprise culture' which centres on customer satisfaction (du Gay and Salaman, 1992). As such, people are driven hard to be enterprising in line with exhortations to develop qualities like self-reliance, boldness and risk taking at the organizational and institutional levels. Eventually this is supposed to remove the reliance on organizations and absolve organizations of blame resulting from tough decisions that involve things like downsizing. An optimistic view would hold that the enterprise culture in fact promotes empowerment and creativity. However, for those who cannot handle the challenges of self-reliance and who lack the requisite skills and confidence, such a culture is seen as punitive.

The culture debate assumed more respectability in the west following the fascination with Asian management values that began with Japanese management and now centres around Chinese management. For Hendry and Pettigrew (1990), HRM was sparked by the 'crisis of confidence' in America in the face of unprecedented Japanese competition. According to this argument, American managers were forced to start addressing the 'softer' parts of the organization which their observations of Japanese management led them to believe offered the answer to their technological, productivity and commitment shortcomings.

HRM thus offered new hope for American industry, which led Guest (1990) to contend that HRM was the latest manifestation of the 'American dream'. The perceived threat to America's competitiveness posed by Japanese firms saw hordes of American executives heading to Japan to unravel the secrets of the Japanese 'miracle' in the 1980s. The obsession with Japanese management was further fuelled by publications that extolled the virtues of the Japanese approach, from *kaizen* (continuous improvement) and 'zero defects' to quality circles and lifetime employment.

23

The dynamism and amazing scope for self-invention in the orient has continued to pose a threat to western capitalist practices. The so-called Asian economic miracle of the 1980s which saw countries like Thailand and South Korea emerge from near economic stagnation into vibrant players on the world stage is a case in point. The subsequent dramatic collapse of the 'tiger economies', while serving as a necessary correction from the excesses of the 1980s, will probably eventually be followed by a new phase of growth, more sustainable and less reckless than the previous one. These events have engendered renewed interest in what exactly makes Asian management tick. Many studies in the genre have been posing a question for which there appears to be no clear answer: what is the role of culture?

Those interested more specifically in China have been struggling to unravel concepts like *guanxi* and face. Thus, although business success in Asia is the outcome of a wide range of industrial, institutional and cultural factors (e.g. Whitley, 1992), the more direct message managers are getting is: if you can understand Asian culture in its various manifestations, you can do business in Asia (e.g. Hampden-Turner and Trompenaars, 1997). To many western managers, understanding the culture is thus the key to neutralizing the threat from the east in order to capitalize on the opportunities available.

The unitarist undertone

From an inducement–contribution perspective, HRM exists to serve a dual objective: to serve the interests of the two key stakeholders – the organization and the individual (among others) – in the first instance. In reality, HRM emerged along fairly unitarist lines, unitarist because of its underlying logic of a perceived congruence of interests and the assumption that all the members of the organization 'should' be working for the good of the firm. This is further elaborated by the shift from collective to individual arrangements. By denying the existence of multiple interests and hence the potential for conflict, this conception of HRM purports to jettison the political dimension – a paradox, since the rise of HRM has itself been a political exercise.

Guest (1989) suggested that the unitarist ethos of HRM was

24

incompatible with the pluralist ethos of industrial relations, which led him to conclude that if HRM brought with it a new set of enlightened practices, it was not clear what role would be left for unions. Foulkes (1980: 12/13) advanced the non-union view by asserting that his framework of analysis which covered non-union firms can be seen as 'the beginnings of a "theory of nonunionization", that, in some ways, is the reverse of a theory of union organization, or, more positively, as a theory of the management of human resources'.

In the UK, Legge (1995) reports the decline in union membership and density, and a decline in trade union recognition. Kochan *et al.* (1986) contend that American managers have a deeply embedded anti-union sentiment, which has been accentuated by the opening of greenfield sites coupled with the closure of union sites. In my own previous research I found that HRM was perceived in some quarters in Kenya as 'an attempt to break unions' (Kamoche, 2000a: 52), while in Thailand, managers are 'at best tolerant of, and at worst vehemently opposed to unions' (Kamoche, 2000b: 454). The notion that HRM is an expedient substitute for trade unions does indeed resonate with many managers around the world and is reflected in the changing face of industrial relations.

The crystallization of HRM?

The foregoing has attempted to piece together some subthemes which depict some of the forces that have shaped HRM thinking in the recent past. The forces that shape HRM cannot of course be defined fully in a few pages. In any case HRM is always changing and evolving as researchers and practitioners discover or invent new strands, concepts, fads and fashions. The metamorphosis will no doubt go on well into the future. A lot has been said about the origins of HRM, and how it supposedly differs from previous forms of labour regulation, e.g. personnel management, industrial relations etc. While it is hardly radical to claim that a committed, well-trained and well-looked after workforce will be more productive and valuable than one that is treated as just another factor of production, HRM as commonly understood has given a new shape and form to the quest to enhance organizational performance through 'human capital'.

Beaumont (1992) suggests, however, that many of the key dimensions of the HR 'movement' are not new – they have been around for many years, through various schools of thought such as human relations and contingency theory. At the beginning of this chapter we traced an even lengthier history. To Mabey *et al.* (1998: 37), what is new 'is not the quality of the ideas but their power. Senior managers are now taking these ideas seriously'. Indeed, HRM is said to have been taken on board by senior management and line managers, and is no longer the domain of personnel departments, especially where it involves issues like training and career development (e.g. Storey, 1992). It remains to be seen, however, whether the motives underpinning this take-up are in the best interests of those for whom the initiatives are undertaken. The following chapters will hopefully shed some light on this.

3

THE EMERGENCE OF 'STRATEGIC HRM'

In this chapter we consider the contribution of debates about the 'strategic' nature of human resource management in order to understand better how managers and researchers have construed the 'value' attributable to the human resource. The notion of 'strategic human resource management' (SHRM) first assumed prominence in the mid-1980s when academics and consultants began to claim that the management of people could be a source of competitive advantage. The quest for the supposedly transformative effects of 'strategy' owes much of its rationale to the levels of competition witnessed in the early 1980s. The quest for 'competitive advantage' received an enormous impetus from the writings of Michael Porter (e.g. 1980).

Interest in strategy and the search for competitive advantage subsequently permeated the key managerial functions such as manufacturing (e.g. Hayes and Wheelwright, 1984) and marketing (Day and Wensley, 1983). Competitive advantage was also being claimed for information technology (Porter and Millar, 1985; Earl, 1989), time (Stalk, 1988), culture (Barney, 1986), and so forth. It was not too long before HR writers joined the bandwagon. If other functions were making a strategic contribution to the organization, it stood to reason that the 'human resource' could also be tapped into for the same purpose. Alternatively, it

27

could be argued that HR practitioners had no choice but to try to demonstrate the strategic value of their function or risk corporate obsolescence. While the idea of managing resources *strategically* is not without some sinister connotations as noted in the 'hard' HRM model – for a critique, see for example Legge (1995) – some might argue that in a way it also represented the beginning of a better appreciation of the potential value of human capital. Accordingly, strategic HRM offered an opportunity to demonstrate the value of a phenomenon which was struggling for recognition as it evolved in a managerial function which some treated with derision. This opportunity emerged in a number of forms:

- it would allow HR managers and academics to distinguish their concerns from those of the perceived low-status 'personnel management';
- it would pave the way for a demonstration of the actual benefits derivable from managing people, thus redefining the contribution to organizational performance;
- it would allow HR practitioners and academics to achieve the status then enjoyed by other 'strategic' players.

Within the field of HRM, the potential for competitive advantage was constructed in a number of ways. For example, Hendry and Pettigrew (1986) argued that in addition to instituting a coherent approach to planning, designing and managing personnel systems, SHRM also entailed a new way of thinking, which saw people as a 'valued resource' and investment. This was essentially a call to acknowledge the value of people's contribution to organizational success. For Tichy *et al.* (1982) a strategic approach to HRM would involve, inter alia, selection and promotion systems, internal flows of people and having the appropriate managerial expertise. Sisson (1989) identified a number of definitive features, such as integrating personnel policies both with one another and with business planning; senior line managers taking responsibility for personnel decisions; a shift from collective to individual arrangements, and an emphasis on commitment. The notion of integration of policies is also a central feature of Guest's (1987) model; Guest also identifies commitment, flexibility and quality. The strategic management of people is now reckoned to be highly problematic due to the conception of strategy, the financial demands of corporations and how

these square with the needs of employees (see also Purcell and
Ahlstrand, 1994; Legge, 1995).

The preoccupation with achieving 'fit'

Initially, the proponents of SHRM argued that HRM strategies had
to find a suitable fit with specific business strategies (e.g. Tichy *et
al.*, 1982; Miles and Snow, 1984; Hendry and Pettigrew, 1986;
Schuler, 1989). This gave birth to the so-called 'matching model of
SHRM', as exemplified by Fombrun *et al.* (1984). In its short history, SHRM has come to be defined largely in terms of matching
HR and business strategy. Hence, it is by claiming an association
with the all-important concept of business strategy that the field
of HR has sought legitimacy, where legitimacy is about being perceived as engaging in actions that are desirable, appropriate and
which enhance reputation (e.g. Suchman, 1995; Galang *et al.*,
1999). In these terms, HRM could in fact be said to have generated
a legitimacy crisis through its role in realizing anorexic organizations. The idea of a 'fit' arises from a key definitive element of
HRM noted above – achieving integration between HR and other
policy areas and in particular with business strategy.

   This has led many researchers to identify ways in which this 'fit'
can actually be realized, and the ways in which specific dimensions of HR support business/corporate strategy. Wright and
Snell (1998) suggest that researchers have sought to fit strategy
with three generic conceptual variables: HRM practices, employee
skills and employee behaviours. Building on this notion of 'fit',
they then proceed to develop a model which dichotomizes 'fit'
and 'flexibility' with regard to how the firm fits the three variables
to the dictates of strategy on the one hand, and how it responds to
other competitive needs not directly dictated by the current strategy. In a sense, therefore, while recognizing that it is helpful to
look at what skills and behavioural repertoires exist within HR
before considering the dictates of the current strategy, their model
still remains firmly wedded to the notion of a 'fit'. The quest for
'fit' has become a fundamental plank in the SHRM models, especially among North American authors.

   Seeking a fit sounds like a meaningful starting point, but it should be realized that there is more to managing people than aligning one's approach to some strategy which is likely to change at short notice. It is doubtful whether any fit would fully capture the nebulous elements inherent in the social context of business, such as employee commitment, politics, the diversity of interests held by the relevant stakeholders and so forth. Also, it is not realistic to expect that people will always behave in the way the model predicts they will. So the best we can expect from this approach to SHRM is some degree of stability in the process of implementing strategy.

The shortcomings of the matching model and similar approaches have been well documented (see for example Boxall, 1992; Mabey and Salaman, 1995; Tyson, 1995). However, although it has become fashionable to dismiss this school of thought largely on the basis that it has not been borne out in reality, this concept deserves credit for focusing researchers' and managers' minds on the need to tap into hitherto unacknowledged human *resource* pools. This point has been ignored by critics who are quick to dismiss HRM as 'sheer rhetoric'. As noted above, this has been an important contribution to the HRM debate: the possibility that people can add value and hence enhance organizational performance. Of course this is not an entirely revolutionary idea. Managers have always known that their profits arise at least in part from the combinations of skills and competencies at their disposal and how these are utilized in productive activities.

Also, it will be recalled that as far back as the 1970s, the proponents of the human resource accounting model tried to express this value in financial terms. Their efforts did not go far enough, and their emphasis on financial worth did not sufficiently capture the tacit nature of skills and competencies, let alone the complexity of the socio-political context of deploying skills. In this regard, the mainstream strategic HR debate appears not to have learned from the errors of the human resource accounting model. This is unfortunate.

It is now generally recognized that matching HR strategies to business strategies is too simplistic an approach. Furthermore, it relegates HR to the role of merely following, rather than driving strategy. Various writers have subsequently recognized that HR strategy and business strategy *can* coexist in a mutually reciprocal

30

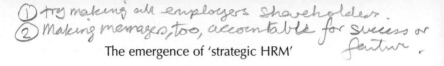

① try making all employers shareholders.
② Making managers, too, accountable for success or failure.

relationship. For example, Lengnick-Hall and Lengnick-Hall (1988) argued that such an approach was superior to one in which human resources are managed primarily as a way to address competitive issues. In a mutually reciprocal relationship, HR issues derive from the existing strategy configuration while at the same time offering scope within which new strategies can be formulated and existing ones reconfigured. Ultimately this means finding a way for human resources to drive the business strategy proactively as opposed to merely supporting it. This is not as far-fetched as it sounds if we think of it as follows: managers would ask themselves not merely what profile of skills, competencies and abilities they need to achieve predetermined strategies, but also what the existing and potentially available stocks of expertise can do to take the organization forward in new directions. To take an analogy from sports, a coach may not always have to resort to 'buying' new players; a good coach should also be asking 'What winning tactics or strategies can I develop with the available talent?' This line of enquiry is pursued further in the following chapter.

HRM and organizational performance

It should be pointed out, however, that the idea that HR *can* drive strategy has been one of the most difficult challenges for the proponents of SHRM. In the following chapter we explore how this might be achieved. This has been particularly difficult in light of the culture of entrenchment and downsizing which has characterized much of the industrial world in the last decade. Many observers now recognize that there is a need to move beyond the rhetoric and to demonstrate that HR *does* generate value and *is* a source of competitive advantage. Ulrich (1997) for example argues that HR executives can no longer go on talking abstractly and conceptually about morale, turnover and commitment; as such, concepts should now be replaced with 'evidence', 'ideas with results' and 'perceptions with assessments'.

Earlier efforts to demonstrate an enhanced role for HRM looked at the extent to which HR managers/executives are involved in strategic planning, and how HR issues are perceived and treated at the highest levels. There has over the years been a marked shift in attitudes about the potential contribution of the HR function in spite of the fact that much of the earlier evidence suggested that HR issues are treated pragmatically and opportunistically (see for example Sisson and Sullivan, 1987; Purcell and Ahlstrand, 1989). This is perhaps best typified by downsizing to eliminate excess capacity, a direct response to specific business strategies like mergers/acquisitions.

By the end of the 1980s, Lengnick-Hall and Lengnick-Hall (1988: 468) captured the prevailing mood by declaring that there was 'little empirical evidence to suggest that strategic HR directly influences organizational performance or competitive advantage'. The stage was thus set for rigorous quantitative analyses to test these claims. This research paradigm has been underpinned by the rationale that the purpose of HR, or any other managerial activities for that matter, is to enhance firm performance, and that this particular interest is predominant (see also Brewster, 1999).

This approach has also, according to Guest (1997), achieved statistical sophistication at the expense of theoretical rigour. Brewster (1999) explains this research tradition in terms of the sharp contrast between the 'universalist paradigm' and the 'contextual paradigm'. While the former uses a nomothetic approach which involves using evidence to test generalizations and which ultimately tends towards the acceptance of convergence, the latter uses an ideographic approach to appreciate what is contextually unique, and why. Put bluntly, universalists search for links between aspects of HRM and firm performance, while contextualists are more concerned to explain any such links.

Strategic HRM has been dominated by 'universalists' who are concerned with what works and, for our purposes here, whether HRM is correlated with firm performance. Subsequently, claims for and against have emerged in an uneasy coexistence. In a review of the 'fit' literature, Wright and Snell (1998) recently found results to be far from conclusive. Mueller (1996) contends that 'proofs' are notoriously shaky: they may be attributable to managerial interests, managerial rhetoric, wishful thinking and erroneous analysis. There is an emergent view now that HR is a potential source of competitive advantage though not necessarily within the context of the traditional 'fit' model. In an earlier piece, Huselid (1995) found less support for the traditional HR–strategy fit, and more support for a 'best practices' approach, i.e. one whereby HR is related to organizational performance irrespective of the strategy chosen. This view has been echoed more recently in Pfeffer's (1998) argument that it is possible to design a set of HR practices which will positively affect performance across all strategies; the challenge is to implement them in an appropriate manner.

More evidence is reported in a 1996 special issue of the *Academy of Management Journal*. For example, Delaney and Huselid (1996) found that while certain administrative HR systems were positively related to various organizational performance indicators, this had more to do with the manufacturing strategy than HR *per se*. Welbourne and Andrews (1996) take a more innovative approach that examines differences between firms that survive and those that fail. One of the most interesting findings they came up with was that surviving firms held strong beliefs about the strategic value of their human resources; they also designed reward systems linked to organizational performance. In the same volume, Becker and Gerhart (1996) caution that empirical research is unlikely to demonstrate clear-cut, unambiguous links between HR practices and firm performance. They also make the timely warning that if indeed HR systems are a source of competitive advantage, aggressive outsourcing may seriously compromise the long-term ability to compete.

This is an important observation which highlights the potential damage that may result from a systematic erosion of the human resource stocks – skills and abilities as well as morale and organizational commitment. As organizations position themselves as leaner and meaner entities, there is always the danger of losing good people through erroneous lay-offs and 'voluntary retirement'. Those remaining also face more pressure for productivity and increased workloads. It does not inspire confidence and a sense of belonging if employees are constantly worrying about whether they will be the victims of the next wave of job cuts. The intangible (e.g. morale, insecurity, adversarial labour relations, etc.) and tangible (e.g. loss of valued competencies) consequences of such actions must be weighed against the more conspicuous financial benefits.

We do not need rocket science statistical analysis to discover that ruthless downsizing and outsourcing are likely to dampen morale and erode job security to the point that dysfunctional turnover ultimately jeopardizes the firm's competitiveness. In this regard we clearly need more research into the real effects of the stock of human resources on organizational performance. The challenge for researchers is to shift their emphasis away from only those things they can measure, which has been the tendency so far. Similarly, they must be prepared to find other organizational outcomes against which to judge the HR initiatives and activities. Financial performance is not the only indicator of organizational performance. Organizations operate in a number of constituencies and respond to the demands of a multiplicity of stakeholders. The stakeholders also affect either directly or indirectly the organizational strategies and their impact cannot therefore be ignored. Stakeholders like employees, customers and pressure groups are becoming more vocal, which suggests a need for managers to move faster toward developing multidimensional approaches to organizational effectiveness than has been the case so far.

Measures of financial performance may serve the interests of shareholders well but do not necessarily tell us how well the organization has responded to its customers in terms of delivering affordable and high-quality goods and services, neither do they convey anything about compliance with regulatory requirements or job-creation and environmental responsibilities. These activities also depend, at least to some extent, on the organization's ability to utilize its stock of human resources effectively. An additional shortcoming of the current studies is that they refer predominantly to profit-making organizations. Their measures would have little relevance to public sector institutions and other organizations like schools in which the generation of an operating surplus is secondary to the provision of a viable education.

It matters . . . it matters not . . .

The debate about the 'value' of human resources is likely to continue into the foreseeable future. There are no doubt many scholars who continue to be fascinated by these questions and who are engaged in studies to investigate the value of human resources as well as the relationships between HR and organizational performance. The question we must now ask is why and for whom does it matter? Why should it matter that HR is a source of competitive advantage? Does it matter to employees that they are perceived as a source of competitive advantage? Let us examine the issue from a different angle – by looking at how managers deal with an activity which, though largely intangible, is believed to impact organizational performance in some way. Managers set aside large advertising budgets because they believe that the resultant exposure their products/services receive generates revenues way above the advertising outlays.

It is not too difficult to analyse the relationships between actual amounts spent and the resultant changes, if any, in revenue. However, does correlation imply causality? Can we really be sure that the effects of other potentially more powerful factors have been isolated and fully accounted for? Such doubts must, inevitably, remain. Nevertheless, such a relationship is considered tenable largely because researchers and managers believe that both advertising and revenue figures are objectively measurable and that the firm has a reasonable amount of control over the design and implementation of the advertising programme. In effect, they *own* the resources and can manipulate them the way they deem fit. Equally important is the underlying rationale that the advertising budget is treated as an *investment*. I have developed this analogy at length because it has some important implications for the treatment of the HRM-organizational performance debate.

There are a number of controversial points, such as how to measure HR initiatives which do not involve specific monetary outlays, or where the administrative costs of systematizing procedures are miniscule *vis-à-vis* the potential gains. These include formalizing systems and processes, e.g. procedures relating to recruitment, training and performance management. Similarly, many HR outcomes are basically intangible and do not easily lend themselves either to objective observation at the very least, or to rigorous measurement. A change in management style and attitudes, improvements in communications, trust, grievance procedures, fairness in promotion decisions and so forth can result in substantial increases in morale and organizational commitment, which may or may not culminate in productivity improvements,

35

i.e. organizational performance. These HR changes might appear inconsequential and yet they might result in a more long-term effect on overall productivity than more conspicuous actions like doubling the training budget.

Many actions such as the ones cited above are basically perceptual, which implies they are likely to be interpreted in different ways depending on who is doing the observing. A supposed improvement in fairness, for example relating to promotion, may not necessarily be visible to unsuccessful candidates. An even more contentious problem is that of causality: with what degree of confidence can we attribute changes in organizational performance to the contributions of HR? As with advertising, in the absence of conclusive multidimensional evidence, it seems such a causality has to be accepted, at least in part, on faith.

This indeed appears to be the case. In spite of the fact that managers do not have such conclusive evidence, many have readily embraced the idea of investing in people, which in some countries like Britain allows them the chance to secure certification attesting to their commitment to training. One wonders whether the quest for certification is driven wholly by the need to communicate a genuine commitment to developing people or a desire to be seen to be so inclined because it sends out a message to relevant stakeholders in a fashion similar to acquiring International Organization Standards (ISO) certification: it serves a pragmatic business purpose.

Yet another angle on this debate is the possibility that the doubts that inevitably surround HR-performance claims may be discouraging sceptical managers from making investments in HR. The question sceptics might be asking is: if there is no proof that HR has any real effect on the bottom line, why invest in people over and above what is necessary to keep them productive? If managers are to be impressed with findings that HR *does* in fact impact organizational performance, it might be expected that they will really begin to believe the cliché that 'human resources are our most important asset'. Undoubtedly, there are those who believe it and act on it – the popular literature is replete with anecdotal reports of such incidences.

Many observers were mesmerized by the discovery of 'excellence' as first postulated by Peters and Waterman (1982). This book marked a watershed in the management debate about what constitutes superior performance and in particular for our purposes the role of the so-called 'soft' aspects of the organization such as culture, attitudes, management style and HRM. The 'excellence movement' thus served as a wake-up call for executives who had never before given more than cursory attention to the possibility that the management of people could generate added value.

Subsequently, a number of firms such as Hewlett-Packard, Johnson and Johnson, GE, Matsushita, etc. came to be associated with that unique 'people-friendly' culture that had been so lauded in the 'excellence movement'. These better-known examples appear to be the exception, yet the extent to which they recur in HRM texts implies a greater prevalence than is perhaps the case. However, by serving as an exemplar, they demonstrate what can be achieved by sophisticated HRM where HR policies are interwoven with core organizational values as part of the business strategy. While there are some reports in the literature about the enhanced role of the human resource function in certain strategic decisions such as mergers and acquisitions, there is scope to research the extent to which managers treat HR as an asset.

Managers have in general adopted a pragmatic approach in aligning human resource strategies to business/corporate strategies. Purcell (1989: 90) paints a pessimistic picture by arguing that trends in corporate strategy, particularly in diversified companies where the prime concern is 'financial economies', 'render the ideals of human resource management . . . unobtainable'. As such, the fact that executives have 'discovered' human resources should not generate undue optimism as to the 'strategic' value with which they are likely to associate HRM.

The question of why the HR-performance debate matters also raises an important issue: will evidence of strong positive associations between HR practices and organizational performance place more pressure on managers to adopt these practices? This assumes that managers were previously neglecting, for example, to provide training because they did not believe it had any meaningful impact on the bottom line. While this may be true, it may also be the case that many managers tend to think of training as an avoidable cost, one which can be minimized by hiring

37

people who will not require much training once deployed on the job. This might in turn explain why firms might want to 'poach' highly qualified people, and also why the provision of firm-specific skills is such an important element in training. Firm-specific skills limit the transferability of skills and may ultimately reduce the individual's marketability.

There are cases where managers are unwilling to release staff to attend training courses because of the pressures of work. While managers are right to be wary of useless courses, it is possible that some are well aware of the potential benefits but choose to ignore them because of other demands with more immediate financial implications. It seems reasonable to assume, therefore, that the *indirect* nature of the impact of many HR initiatives on firm performance is likely to discourage decision makers from giving such initiatives the attention they seem to deserve in the face of competing demands and scarce resources. This problem is compounded further by worries about retention and appropriation.

The issue of retention is a straightforward one: can the firm retain effective performers and contain dysfunctional turnover? This has not received exhaustive attention in the literature. Some authors, however, have attempted to link retention to business strategy. For example, Siehl and Smith (1990) suggest that in mergers and acquisitions, the retention of managers should be linked to the acquisition strategy. This signals a form of selective retention, which can be considered to typify the basic rationale underpinning employee retention: firms will seek to retain high performers and attempt to transform or deselect low performers. They will first ensure they can retain high performers before they can appropriate the added value attributed to these individuals. This issue is dealt with in more detail in Chapter 5. We argue here that the firm's ability to design mechanisms to retain productive employees and channel their capabilities towards the achievement of business strategies is a starting point towards realizing the strategic value of human resources.

Appropriation is a much more complex problem. Simply stated, appropriation is about the firm's ability to retain the benefits from utilizing its resources (e.g. Kay, 1995). Within HRM, as Kamoche (1996a) and Kamoche and Mueller (1998) have argued, this becomes more problematic because the firm does not necessarily

[handwritten margin note: governance structures – legally binding requirements on employees e.g. length of service.]

have proprietorial rights over its employees. By implication, its claims to possess such rights over the knowledge attributable to employees are not necessarily a *fait accompli*. This is why firms find it necessary to institute protective governance structures over the use of skills and competencies.

Simply retaining people is not good enough. It has to be understood that people possess something of value, and the task of the manager is to draw this out, and to create an environment in which the employees are able to realize this value. We deal with these issues in subsequent chapters. For our purposes here, suffice it to note that doubts about the firm's ability to retain employees and, perhaps more importantly, the capacity to retain the benefits from utilizing their skills are factors that are likely to mediate the HRM–organizational performance interface.

Therefore, even though managers might be presented with irrefutable 'proof' that HR initiatives and practices contribute to the achievement of the firm's business strategies, the retention and appropriation problems might discourage managers from making extra efforts to invest in more innovative HRM activities. Fears are likely to linger about whether the employees receiving developmental investments, particularly in training, will stay with the firm long enough for the firm to recoup the investment. This is indeed one of the most commonly cited problems by managers worldwide. A recent survey reported in the *Financial Times* (Anderson, 2000) found that one-third of all MBA students in the UK leave their companies within a year of graduating. For many of them the failure of the organization to provide challenging work was a key reason for this loss of talent. This raises serious concerns about the whole issue of investing in people. Training for the sake of training can often have dire consequences which eventually discourage further training while feeding a self-fulfilling prophesy that HR does not add value because people are leaving.

Rather than exploring the opportunities for better utilizing the new skills, organizations tend to lock people into the system. It is not uncommon, for example, for organizations to require managers to work for a predetermined number of years after receiving sponsorship to take an MBA degree. Some universities impose similar conditions on staff receiving sponsorship to take higher degrees. Universities in some Asian countries such as Thailand exemplify a more extreme case by requiring staff to work for up to three times the number of years they received the sponsorship; thus a four-year PhD programme could result in a twelve-year lock-in. Such governance structures serve the purpose of securing retention but do not necessarily assure appropriation. It is argued further here that such protective governance mechanisms cannot act as a surrogate for deriving a competitive edge from the management of people. There is an additional paradox here: people in these sorts of situations do not necessarily treat the governance structure as a form of 'job security'.

People as a strategic resource: a neglected view

So far we have considered how researchers and practitioners have construed the value inherent in people. In this section we consider a hitherto neglected question: do employees consider their contribution valuable, or indeed a source of competitive advantage? The views of the real subjects in the HRM–performance debate are conspicuous by their absence. This is mainly because research in this genre is hardly ever directed at employees themselves but treats managers/supervisors as the key informants. Perhaps due to fears about the leakage of confidential information or disclosure of sensitive data, managers granting permission for research often prohibit access to ordinary employees. Many research projects are also designed in such a way that the nature of information sought is only available from senior management. Other researchers probably believe that the higher up the organizational hierarchy are their respondents, the more legitimate the findings.

This is perhaps attributable to the top-down structure of strategy formulation and the implicit assumption that those at the lower echelons cannot be expected to have an opinion on strategic matters. As such, methodology sections of many articles state that 'questionnaires were sent to (or interviews were held with) the CEOs of Fortune 500 . . .' The veracity of research findings cannot always be guaranteed and concerns have been raised about busy executives delegating the form-filling to subordinates. What is now needed is a broader perspective in research design and data collection. Researchers also need to be prepared to develop innovative approaches for analysing the diversity of human resource questions and to be more adventurous (see also Napier and Vu, 1998). On the part of managers, there clearly needs to be a greater willingness to grant access to their subordinates in these sorts of studies.

While the views of employees are missing, their expectations have received plenty of attention from scholars in management. This attention (and sometimes speculation) relates to what researchers expect people want, and how the satisfaction of employee needs/expectations can be aligned to the achievement of organizational objectives, ultimately leading to competitive advantage through the logic of the 'matching' principle. This approach finds expression in contemporary debates about the new psychological contract – what it means, how it can be sustained, how it comes to be violated (e.g. Robinson *et al.*, 1994; Rousseau, 1995; Morrison and Robinson, 1997), and how it is often sustained through managerial rhetoric (e.g. Grant, 1999).

As noted earlier, the reality of the employment relationship revolves very much around what the two parties bring to the bargaining table. In this regard, Hiltrop (1995) argues that the employee will be employed to the extent that he/she adds value and finds new ways to add value to the organization, and that 'in return, the employee has the right to demand interesting and important work, has the freedom and resources to perform it, receives pay that reflects his or her contribution, and gets the experience and training needed to be employable . . .' No doubt employees want interesting work, reasonable pay, a good working environment and so forth. The implications of these requirements were clearly spelt out in the earliest theories of motivation. But the world has changed, as have the nature and meaning of work, employment relationships and people's aspirations.

Most of the research that seeks to address this question has been concerned with the effect of management actions/strategies/ styles etc. on employee behaviour. Such studies include the effect of management style on employee commitment, with findings suggesting that effective two-way communications and participative decision making lead to higher commitment (e.g. Morris and Steers, 1980). These kinds of findings are hardly surprising. What is remarkable is that they take a deliberate managerialist view to define what factors or outcomes are considered desirable, and for whom – in this case, commitment is deemed to be an important outcome for the organization.

We still do not know why or whether managerially defined outcomes like commitment should matter to the employee, especially in an era in which people are increasingly worried about job security, and their own survival. The scenario is compounded further by employee perceptions of a lack of reciprocity in the commitment equation: organizations are demanding and increasingly failing to offer commitment in the form of job security, for example. In fact the very relevance of the concept of organizational commitment is now being questioned, given current trends in corporate downsizing (e.g. Baruch, 1988). While recognizing that multiple forms of commitment exist, Mowday (1998: 394) also notes that the frequency of mergers today 'makes one wonder whether employees know from one day to the next who they are working for, let alone what organization they are committed to, if any'.

This suggests the need for a radically new approach to researching HRM by going beyond the simple model that takes a unidimensional view of the HRM–performance interface. Such an approach could start by asking people how they perceive their place in the organizational context, what abilities they possess, the value they attach to their abilities and potential contribution and what kind of situational context would best allow them to realize their abilities in line with the business strategies. This is currently found to some extent in progressive career development-oriented performance appraisal techniques. There appears to be a strong case for more research into the viability of such an approach. The basic premise would be one in which the two protagonists in the HRM–organizational goals interface come closer to a partnership that works to forge a mutually beneficial relationship. In the next chapter, we examine the extent to which recent developments in strategic HRM address this issue.

4

THE CONTRIBUTION OF THE RESOURCE-BASED VIEW

The rediscovery of the resource-based view (RBV) of the firm was arguably the high point of the strategic HRM debate in the mid-1990s. This rapprochement between strategic management and HRM promised to inject new thinking into the strategic HRM debate and to pave the way for a more meaningful research agenda into the ways in which HRM can serve as a source of sustainable competitive advantage. In this chapter we re-examine the rationale behind the RBV, identify its constitutive elements and ponder the question as to why some researchers believed (and continue to believe) in the superior value of the RBV *vis-à-vis* other analytical perspectives. We then proceed to examine the extent to which this perspective has informed the theory and practice of HRM, and what shortcomings, if any, have prevented the full realization of the benefits promised by the emergence of this perspective.

From the industrial to the resource-based view of the firm

The quest for strategic advantage has for a long time been underpinned by the assumption that firm superiority is demonstrated through outperforming rivals out in the market. This logic is defined within the scenario of industrial competition with firms striving to gain market share and produce better quality goods and services at a better price than competitors. Hence the notion of 'competitive advantage'. Michael Porter (e.g. 1985) has been one of the most ardent proponents of this perspective. Porter has made a substantial contribution particularly in his writings about the way firms compete through a choice of strategies like differentiation, cost and niche, and in his popularization of constructs such as the 'value chain'. Many people, in academia, business and consultancy, have taken some of these ideas at face value in their quest for 'competitive advantage'.

Constructs like the value chain, portfolio analysis and so forth have also been stretched to their absolute limits in strategic management both in practice and in classroom case study analysis. We thus hear of business units or subsidiaries being treated as 'stars', 'cash cows' or 'dogs' (for a critique, see Purcell, 1989). In the previous chapter we noted how 'strategic' has over the years come to preface every other managerial function. The industrial organization perspective has no doubt increased our understanding of the dynamics of competition. However, some of the 'theories' and practices it has, perhaps inadvertently, spawned are of doubtful value in clarifying the nature of strategic HRM.

One such outcome is the notion of 'matching' business strategy to HR practice. Without rehearsing the concomitant arguments in the previous chapter, we note here that this approach works on the assumption that there already exist certain strategies which will then be matched in a semi-mechanistic fashion to specific, codified HRM practices. What is problematic about this scenario is that the strategies are taken as given. They exist out there, although we are not told about the process of their formulation, and the task for the manager is merely to implement them. As Mueller (1996) has pointed out, there is insufficient theoretical and empirical justification for the preoccupation with explicitly formulated, codified HRM practices.

The current tendency assumes a high degree of rationality on the part of the decision maker, who is expected to look *outside* the organization at what rival firms are doing in order to determine how his/her organization should (re)act. The external competitive environment is viewed as the source of opportunities to generate added value. The source of growth exists out there in the market. This is in contrast with the RBV of the firm which suggests that the source of such value should be sought within the firm's own internal environment, in particular in the configuration of internally held resources as well as in the industry.

Edith Penrose (e.g. 1959) is generally considered as one of the originators of this concept, although this line of thinking is traceable as far back as Coase (1937). Penrose's postulations were to remain more or less dormant for twenty years before they started to re-emerge in the early 1980s. Some earlier contributions that seem pertinent to the debate include Nelson and Winter (1982), Teece (1982) and Rumelt (1984). However, it was Wernerfelt's (1984) seminal paper which fully relaunched the debate. Penrose viewed the firm as 'an administrative organization and a collection of productive resources' (1959: 24), or 'a bundle of potential services' (1959: 25). According to her analysis, the nature and configuration of resources differs from firm to firm, which means that firms must be treated as 'heterogeneous'. This perspective stands in sharp contrast to the neoclassical claim of firm homogeneity within industries which is supposedly realizable through inter-firm competition.

As such, competition does not eliminate all differences among firms because all firms are inherently unique by virtue of differential resource endowment. This uniqueness therefore becomes a potentially robust source of competitive advantage. Scholars suggest, however, that the bundle of resources does not automatically confer competitive advantage on the firm. To do so, the resources must satisfy certain conditions: they must be rare (scarce), inimitable, non-substitutable and appropriable (e.g. Barney, 1991; Grant, 1991a; Amit and Schoemaker, 1993). Upon fulfilling these conditions, resources can then be understood as 'valuable' within the context of performing productive activities that are at the heart of the organization's strategy (Kamoche, 1996a). This is an important test of what is considered valuable and why.

In and of themselves, resources are only potentially valuable; their real value becomes manifest when they are applied to activities that allow them to provide a service. As Penrose argued, unutilized or underutilized resources constitute new opportunities

45

for growth. Therefore, as long as there remain resources whose use is currently not being optimized, an 'opportunity cost' can be inferred. The same applies to resources that are either 'misused' or being used inappropriately. This may appear obvious in the case of financial and physical assets. It is contended here that a similar situation obtains with regard to human resources. Skills and competencies that are allowed to remain idle constitute a cost both to the organization and to the individual. This implies that as long as the full potential of the stock of human capital is not realized, it is meaningless to talk about human resources being the most important assets.

The above conditions (and other similar ones) have been discussed at length in the strategic management literature (e.g. Grant, 1991a, b; Amit and Schoemaker, 1993) and in their application to SHRM (e.g. Wright *et al.*, 1994; Kamoche, 1996a; Mueller, 1996). Within the HRM debate we can think of scarcity in terms of high-quality skills and managerial know-how as opposed to absolute numbers of people. Superior skills and talents would normally be in limited supply. The way such skills are utilized, for example when people work in teams with a high degree of interdependence, can vary a lot from firm to firm even where such skills are fairly similar. An example is in the management of professionals and technical staff with similar training, education and experience. This might explain why merely poaching key performers from rival firms may not result in the desired outcomes.

There are many other things that must be taken into consideration for such moves to work, including putting in place a culture and structure within which the new expertise can be absorbed and allowed to thrive. This calls to mind what Teece (1986) refers to as cospecialized assets. In the HR context if a supportive culture is absent, suitable technology is not in place, or mechanisms for developing and sharing information are not encouraged, then poaching high performers may not serve the intended purpose. Grant (1991a: 127) notes that 'even if the resources that constitute the team are transferred, the nature of organizational routines – in particular, the role of tacit knowledge and unconscious coordination – makes the recreation of capabilities within a new corporate environment uncertain'.

For our purposes, capabilities represent the capacity to deploy resources (see also Amit and Schoemaker, 1993). These may be within the broader context of 'the firm's capacity to secure, nurture, retain and deploy human resources through HR policies and practices' (Kamoche, 1996a: 216). In Grant's terms, HR capabilities would be seen with respect to how skills and expertise are transformed into a strategic competence that allows the organization to achieve its objectives. The competence resulting from the embeddedness of the HR skills within the organizational routines becomes a major source of strength. In the narrower context of changing jobs, the ability of an individual or team to continue delivering superior performance may heavily depend on the existence of a supportive internal environment as well as the individual's ability to transfer the capabilities that previously facilitated superior performance.

For example, the effectiveness of a marketing or advertising executive might depend on whether that individual can retain and use valuable contacts. Similarly, a sports star may experience difficulty in gelling with new teammates or fitting into the new coach's regime, thus constraining his/her effectiveness. These difficulties may only be temporary but they still help to highlight the uniqueness of specialized human resource assets, and the difficulties associated with imitating and substituting them. The significance of this issue is currently receiving attention within the framework of social capital (e.g. Nahapiet and Ghoshal, 1998). The question of appropriation is dealt with in the next chapter.

As Amit and Schoemaker (1993) point out, some invisible assets that are deeply rooted in the organization's history (such as organizational knowledge or trust between management and unions) cannot be traded or easily replicated. The firm-specificity of such assets has to be understood in terms of a long process of accumulation. It takes time to build capabilities that are consonant with the organization's strategic requirements and which have been shown to play a pivotal role in the organization's competitiveness. Such unique capabilities cannot merely be purchased, but have to be built up over time. Dierickx and Cool (1989) refer to this as 'time compression diseconomies'. Competitors may find it extremely difficult to understand how a firm configures its resource stocks, and in particular how the utilization of these resources generates added value. This is referred to as causal ambiguity (e.g. Lippman and Rumelt, 1982; Dierickx and Cool, 1989; Reed and DeFillippi, 1990).

This argument has very important implications for HRM where resources like knowledge, trust, commitment and so forth are by definition intangible and tacit and have to be built up over time. The tradability of such resources appears rather limited: can one buy trust, or commitment? Can an organization hire or poach people who are deemed to be committed? The problems of picking the *right* person in employee selection are particularly pertinent here. The recruiter does not know the extent to which the new hires will be committed to organizational objectives that they have not yet been exposed to. They will have to wait and see, just as they have to nurture trust over a period of time.

In the context of strategic management, Dierickx and Cool (1989) deliberate this point by explaining the weaknesses of the concept of 'strategic factor markets' which according to Barney (1986) is the market in which firms acquire resources necessary to implement a strategy. Dierickx and Cool point out that some resources like trust, loyalty of dealers or customers cannot be bought but must be earned through a history of honest dealings. Japanese companies like Sony, Matsushita, Toyota and others did not buy their reputation for quality; they built it up through continuous improvement over decades from the earliest days when 'Made in Japan' was synonymous with bad quality.

This same argument can equally be applied to HRM: not all aspects of human *resources* can be acquired externally. Of course new staff can be hired directly from the labour market especially those bringing in generic skills, such as fresh university graduates or factory workers. The firm will then want to equip them with firm-specific skills through on-the-job and similar forms of firm-specific training. The effect is to limit the workers' mobility because firm-specific skills may be of limited value to rival firms. The workers may have to be retrained for the new organization's requirements, or have their attitudes and working styles substantially readjusted in order to fit into the new environment. The way in which these firm-specific skills are configured and harnessed to the organizational capabilities and deployed in productive activities is likely to differ widely from firm to firm.

Not only does this potentially accentuate the uniqueness of each firm in Penrosian terms, it also casts further doubt on the appropriateness of looking to the external competitive environment in seeking to derive advantage from human resource management. The relevance of the RBV in the effective management of human resources thus becomes more readily evident. The stock of skills, talents and competencies is tied in with a complex web of other tacit resources in the social context of organizations, including such nebulous constructs as trust and loyalty. It appears reasonable to predict that the complexity of this social context and its implications for organizational performance must be understood first by looking within the organization.

To conclude this discussion, we are suggesting here that the development of strategic HRM models that derive from the orthodox conception of strategic management suffers from some fundamental flaws. This is not to argue that approaches like the 'matching model' have little to offer. The criticism is that such models rest on very shaky conceptual grounds and, as a result, their stipulations for the management of people are necessarily suspect. It should be pointed out, however, that the RBV is not being offered here in way of a complete rejection of the orthodox conceptions of strategic management. Two important points clarify our position: first, it would be unrealistic to discount the importance of the competitive environment in a world in which competition plays such a decisive role in firm survival.

If any proof were needed, this has been amply demonstrated in the turbulent years of a global recession and the subsequent financial crisis which began with the meltdown of Asian economies in 1997. Even as these economies begin to show the first signs of a recovery, global uncertainty continues with the precariousness of the so-called 'new economy' that is now dominated by technological investment and internet stocks. The firm cannot therefore be divorced from the realities of industrial competition and turbulence. Even as she laid the foundation for a theory of internal resource heterogeneity, Penrose recognized that inducements and obstacles to expansion can be found both inside and outside the firm.

In any case, in HRM, the firm has to compete with rivals for high-potential people in the external labour market and only then can it begin to treat their skills and talents as strategic assets in the way it develops them. Therefore, the important contribution of the RBV is to redirect attention toward an environment over which the firm can exercise relative control. The second point is that this is not merely an attempt to promote or advocate the RBV. There has been enough prescription in the literature. My concern here is to take a critical look at the debate to establish why this concept might be of value to HRM, and the extent to which it has informed SHRM research. Hopefully this discussion will bring us closer to an understanding of the essence of human resources, with an emphasis on 'resource'.

The dominance of the external environment

The SHRM/RBV debate is yet to mature. The literature began to emerge in the early 1990s. Cappelli and Singh's (1992) paper was probably one of the first efforts to articulate the relevance of the RB view to strategic HRM via strategic management. Cappelli and Singh conclude their discussion as follows:

> Perhaps the most important element in the research program we propose is the perspective that competitive advantage arises from firm-specific, valuable resources that are difficult to imitate. With this perspective, an important research question relates to the role of human resource policies in the creation of valuable, firm-specific skills. A related question addresses the processes of diffusion or imitation of successful human resource practices across the firms. A core agenda for the future is the development of an empirical base relating human resource policies to rent-generating resources of the firm. Such an empirical base will help develop more refined perspectives on human resource decisions that particularly impact long-term profits earned by the firm.
>
> (Cappelli and Singh, 1992: 186)

The one point that appears to have been taken up is the analysis of rent-generating resources. However, this has been addressed not necessarily as framed within Cappelli and Singh's conception of the RBV but in terms of the financial implications of HR practices, i.e. whether HRM practices affect firm performance. This question has been addressed above. This literature is firmly grounded within the industrial organization model of strategic management.

The impact of the competitive environment especially in times of radical change and turbulence in part accounts for the prevalence of this perspective on studies of HR effectiveness, as in the case of British Airways (Colling, 1995). In this genre, organizations are seen as reacting to an external environment as they struggle to survive. In an earlier contribution, Gunnigle and Moore (1994) conceptualize strategy with regard to the (external) product market, drawing mainly from Michael Porter's work. However, they raise some criticisms about the failure of the external context models to address 'internal context and process issues'. As far as their multinational subsidiaries were concerned they found that many personnel practitioners expected corporate strategy to be determined at the corporate centre with minimal local involvement – it was in the main a 'given'.

In such cases, managers are expected to align their HR practices with strategies they have played little or no role in formulating and which are simply handed down with strict implementation requirements. It is unlikely therefore that such managers would be over-anxious to design practices (let alone 'create' human resources) that are 'inimitable' or 'unsubstitutable'. This probably points to the unrealistic nature of the RBV given existing institutional arrangements and organizational structures. Managers of subsidiary companies or 'strategic business units' in general would have to have a substantial stake in the decision-making and strategy-formulation process if the RBV is to become a reality at the practical level.

Such frontline managers are particularly well placed to understand the diversity of skills and competencies as they are dealing with subordinates on an ongoing basis. This argument parallels the view that line managers should be more involved in human resource decisions given their privileged viewpoint in the workplace and their knowledge of what works and what needs doing. They would have to have sufficient power to determine what resources or combinations of resources should be fostered in order to generate added value, and how their deployment might shape strategy, rather than the other way round. Few organizations are designed to accommodate such a scenario.

From practices to resources

In this section we attempt to refocus attention on the very important aspect of the human *resource*. As noted above, the SHRM research tradition has been heavily influenced by the formal matching model that preceded it. For example, Schuler and Jackson (1987) draw from the dominant strategic management construct of product life cycle phases to assess product market influences on business strategy and personnel policy. The majority of authors are concerned with HR *policies* and *practices* as opposed to the human *resources* as understood within the resource-based view (e.g. Russell *et al.*, 1985; Terpstra and Rozell, 1993; Arthur, 1994; Ulrich, 1997). For a critique see Mueller (1996).

Inherent in these studies is the assumption that there exists a pool of talent and expertise whose characteristics are largely unproblematic; all that is needed is a set of policies and practices to drive the HR pool so that it will 'contribute to the achievement of business strategies and organizational performance'. By conceptualizing HRM only in terms of policies and practices while ignoring the nature and configuration of the knowledge, skills and abilities (KSAs), we are only being presented with a one-dimensional view. As long as the relationship between KSAs and practices remains undefined, subsequent conclusions that HRM does or does not lead to competitive advantage must be treated with scepticism.

One possible exception is Huselid *et al.*'s (1997) broad 'components factor structure' of HRM which includes, inter alia, 'HRM effectiveness' and 'professional capabilities'. The former includes the familiar practices such as compensation, performance appraisal, teamwork, training and so forth. The latter comprises expertise and skills among staff in a human resource functional department: leadership, knowledge of HR functions and rivals' practices, foreign language capability, computer literacy and so forth.

Although these authors recognize the relevance of the RBV to their argument, they relate it to their construct of 'HRM effectiveness' and do not indicate how this concept relates more directly to the 'HR capabilities'. They state, for example, that 'strategic HRM activities . . . help a firm to ensure that its human resources are not easily imitated'. It is not clear from their analysis what it means to imitate resources. They proceed to argue that competitors cannot easily copy HR practices because of 'the social complexity and causal ambiguity inherent in strategic HRM practices' (1997: 173) which suggests that their concern with inimitability in fact relates to the *practices* rather than to the 'HR capabilities'.

The current situation can be characterized as depicting a linear relationship between HR policies/practices and organizational performance. It is suggested here that a more meaningful approach would be to include a conception of 'resources' alongside the formulation of policies/strategies first, and then explore the relationship, if any, with organizational performance. Such an approach would facilitate a fuller understanding of what exactly constitutes the 'resource', which for the sake of argument we characterize here in terms of knowledge, skills and abilities.

Whither the resource-based view?

Despite the advances that have been made in developing the conceptual scope of the RB view, this perspective appears not to have informed much empirical research so far. HRM researchers have either not understood it, or have simply chosen to ignore it. But the concept refuses to go away. Clark (2000) reminds us that for Penrose productive services are to be perceived as part of the managerial expertise. This imposes a limitation on 'Penrosian learning' since, as Mueller (1996) argues, strategic assets are unlikely to result from senior management alone. Instead they are created in an evolutionary fashion over time, an analysis which echoes Dierickx and Cool's (1989) 'time compression diseconomies' – the careful cultivation of resources over a period of time.

In the meantime, the RBV is still enjoying a fascination with theoretical sophistication. The bulk of the literature so far is struggling to unpack the conceptual issues attendant to this new thinking. This is no doubt a useful phase in the maturation of an idea and it is not being suggested here that researchers must now rush off with questionnaires to test the dimensions of the RB view, however valuable such an exercise might be. In this section we consider some aspects of the limited empirical work on the concept within the HRM debate and then reflect on the reasons for the apparent neglect of the RBV by HRM scholars.

An early empirical application of the RB view is found in the analysis of basketball teams by Wright *et al.* (1995). This paper is based on the rationale that in sports, human resources, in particular individuals' skills, have a direct and obvious influence on organizational performance. This is one area in which it is the skills and talents of the team members upon which the very survival of the club hinges. Equally noteworthy is the fact that these skills and talents are essentially tacit. Clearly, skills and talents in a sport as competitive as a basketball league provide an excellent opportunity to examine the connection between human resources (at the level of individual 'employees') and organizational (i.e. team/club) performance. Relating their discussion to business organizations, Wright *et al.* observe that although top managers formulate the strategy and mid-level managers implement it, 'employees who have direct contact with the customers determine the ultimate success of the strategy. If employees do not possess the necessary customer service attitude and skills, it is unlikely that the strategy will be effectively implemented' (1995: 1055).

This study produced some interesting results. For example, the authors found that the match between skills and the coach's strategy determined performance. Certain skills were found to be more strongly related to performance for some coaching strategies than for other strategies. This finding lends support to the view that there is no one best strategy and is consistent with the notion of internal resource heterogeneity and firm uniqueness. According to the authors, the study also provided some 'indirect evidence' that skills play a role in determining strategy. This happened when a coach was unable to implement his 'preferred strategy' and instead chose a different one which was more suited to the stock of available skills. Simply stated, this means that a coach may try to do something new with existing talents rather than merely getting team members to play according to some predetermined formula. Still, we suggest that while coaches might be willing to take a flexible approach in accommodating some of the idiosyncrasies of top-performing maverick players by changing tactics, they are not likely to allow such flexibility to influence their strategies fundamentally.

Outside sports and entertainment, we argue that the scope for *(?)* the above approach is fairly limited but could perhaps be general- *really* ized to situations in which organizations may not possess or have access to the necessary stock of skills in the short term. In other fields like the professions where KSAs have a direct bearing on performance, the organization would normally undertake an aggressive recruitment drive or subcontract the work rather than allow the available skills that may not be very well developed to dictate strategy. In the case of a law firm that specializes in corporate law, we would expect experts who leave to be replaced promptly as opposed to changing track to venture into criminal law, for example, which may not fall squarely into the firm's area of expertise. Some lines of expertise in the professions and technical fields take a long time to develop. Of course scope to diversify could be influenced by the hitherto underutilized areas of expertise as we argued above, and it may be that diversification may involve incremental rather than radical shifts in strategy. This view is consistent with Penrose's argument that currently unused or underutilized resources constitute scope for future growth.

A second paper in this genre is Boxall and Steeneveld's (1999) longitudinal study of human resource management in engineering consultancies. This study examined the extent to which engineering consultancies performed on the basis of superior management of human resources. The longitudinal nature of the study allowed the researchers to focus on the impact of HR strategies on performance over a five-year period. The study demonstrated the critical role that 'contract-winning staff' play in helping engineering consultancies achieve their strategic objectives.

Thus both the basketball and consultancy studies appear to lend credence to the RB view as an analytical paradigm within the HR debate. This is attributable to the fact that in these fields the generation, or accumulation and leveraging of knowledge in effect defines the organization's core activity. It may well be the case that future RBV research within HRM will proceed in fields such as services/professions and sports/entertainment where the role of KSAs might be more readily evident.

Coincidentally, these are areas that have tended to receive comparatively less attention. The neglect of the RBV by HRM researchers is thus attributable (at least partly) to the preoccupation with more traditional organizations such as manufacturing companies and heavy industries (the literature is littered with references to IBM, GM, Toyota etc). The core productive activity in such firms is largely driven by technology, with HR playing a less visible but no doubt crucial role. It is not surprising therefore that the evidence as to the link between HR and firm performance has been so inconclusive. Perhaps researchers are looking in the wrong place!

A second reason could be found in the methodological preference. Resources, in particular intangible ones, should be studied not merely as at a point in time or in terms of immediately observable outcomes but in terms of the process through which they come into being. The idea that the value of resources should be seen within a historical context is an important aspect of the RBV in particular as it relates to intangible assets (Dierickx and Cool, 1989; Mueller, 1996). This has important implications for research methodologies. In this regard, Boxall and Steeneveld (1999: 449) have noted that 'The statistical study of large populations of organizations tends not to provide insights into the thread of critical historical events. As resource-based theory implies, this makes such studies less useful in the analysis of competitive advantage.'

In conclusion we argue that researchers will need to be more innovative both in terms of the industries they select and the methodologies they choose to apply. The suitability of the dominant industrial organization paradigm will continue to be tested against the increasing complexity of the conception of HRM which, as we have noted above, needs to take greater account of the 'resource' part in addition to the practices and policies. Once researchers fully appreciate the complexity of KSAs and devise more appropriate methods for studying them, it will no longer be necessary to invoke the platitude that people are 'our most important asset'. Ultimately, the question as to whether human resources are more important than other resources should matter less than how all these resources are cultivated and utilized in an organization's productive activities. According to Mueller (1996), human resources have to be seen within the context of a firm's broad array of resources. As such, it is helpful for a firm to specify the interdependence of these resources in its productive activities rather than merely distinguish between their supposed relative importance.

In this chapter we examined how the resource-based view has reignited the debate about the conception and significance of the 'human resource'. In the following chapter we turn to the politically problematic issue surrounding the 'use' of this resource.

5

THE DYNAMICS OF APPROPRIATION

Our discussion so far has considered the contemporary debates surrounding the emergence of human resource management. In the previous two chapters we focused more specifically on the contribution from strategic management and the extent to which these developments have enhanced our understanding of the issues at hand. In this chapter we turn to a theoretical perspective which has received even less attention in the HRM literature than the resource-based view but which, it is maintained here, lies at the heart of the employment relationship – appropriation. We consider how this concept helps us to unravel this complex relationship, how it fits in with issues like retention and the extent to which it explains the distribution of benefits – however defined – arising from the utilization of resources.

The basis of appropriation

Appropriation is about securing and retaining the benefits arising from the utilization of resources. In simple economic terms, the benefits represent the 'added value', or 'surplus value' generated from productive activities. The question of appropriation is usually treated as unproblematic within the HRM literature because it is generally assumed that this surplus or added value belongs to the party that *owns* or *controls* the productive resources and means of production – the firm. Kamoche (1996a) and Kamoche and Mueller (1998) have highlighted the weakness of this argument as it relates to HRM where we cannot talk about firms 'owning' people. Whatever accrues to other parties, e.g. suppliers, employees, the government, is deemed payable on the basis of predetermined formulae, contracts or other forms of agreement. Thus, shareholders receive dividends, employees accept predetermined wages, suppliers are paid their dues, and the government receives tax. The broader community might also be allowed to appropriate some of this added value through corporate donations.

The idea that it is the firm that is doing the primary appropriating owes its origins to the strategic management literature where resources are perceived as *belonging* to the firm. For strategic management theorists (who generally prefer the term *appropriability*), appropriation refers to the capacity to achieve the retention and absorption of 'above-normal rates of return or rents'. Coff (1999) points out that the resource-based view was formulated to explain *when firms will appropriate rents*, not *who will appropriate it*. This is reflected in the neglect of the concept of appropriation in the RBV literature. The limited treatment of appropriation within the RBV has basically emphasized the claim that resources must be 'appropriable by the firm'.

For example, Mahoney and Pandian (1992: 364) suggest that the firm may appropriate rents when resources are firm-specific. Kay (1995: 181, emphasis added) states that appropriability is 'the capacity of the firm to retain the added value *for its own benefit*'. He proceeds to argue, however, that the firm will also generally distribute at least some of the returns among various other stakeholders – suppliers, employees, the state and customers. Kay (1995: 190) argues that the degree to which these stakeholders appropriate added value 'is measured by the difference between what they earn, or pay, under the contract they have with the firm and what they would earn, or pay, under the best alternative contract open to them'.

With regard to HRM, this refers primarily to what people earn above their contractual arrangement and also relative to what they would earn elsewhere. The appropriation regime cannot be viewed simply within the context of wages and benefits and needs to be extended to a broader domain which includes such rent-sharing mechanisms as the various forms of profit sharing: stock options, bonuses and performance-based reward systems (e.g. Poole and Jenkins, 1990). Additionally, it must take into account non-tangible outcomes like opportunities for learning and personal development as well as fairness in the distribution of organizational outcomes, tangible and intangible. The question of appropriation therefore revolves around how the wide range of benefits arising from the utilization of human resources are distributed among the relevant stakeholders. The discussion must also take into account the fact that the contractual arrangement under which returns are shared may be questionable.

Examples include cases where people believe themselves to be underpaid compared with colleagues doing similar work, or where the scope for wage bargaining either individually or collectively is either restricted or inherently unfair. Furthermore, it should be recalled that rewards come in a variety of forms – from monetary pay to psychological rewards such as intrinsic satisfaction, opportunities for growth, status and recognition. Clearly, psychological rewards do not fit into the strategic management conception of appropriation – they are not normally part of a formal contractual arrangement – and yet they might be playing a fundamental role in the appropriation regime. In Chapter 6, we extend the debate to the broader concept of knowledge.

Evidently much of the current strategic management literature that touches on appropriation is decidedly unitarist – it only considers the firm's point of view. Interestingly, the *firm* is often perceived in these debates within a purely economic context, as an entity in its own right, as though it had a life of its own. Appropriation of added value thus seems to refer to the scope to reinvest added value in order to continue generating further returns. Grant (1991b: 112) goes a step further by defining appropriability as 'what determines the division of rents between the firm and the owners of the resources'.

This definition is noteworthy since it recognizes that the firm does not necessarily *own* the resources it controls. In particular, Grant cites the specific role of human resources and the fact that individuals – mostly high performers in professional service firms and sports clubs – have a capacity to identify the proportion of rents that is attributable directly to themselves. Such individuals will subsequently lay a claim to these rents, thus demonstrating that the appropriation exercise must proceed in a more pluralistic fashion.

The need to recognize the individual's propensity to appropriate rent is further recognized in those studies that focus on the 'managerial resource'. Agency theory has so far served as the central framework for theorizing the nature of contracts between managers and the firm (e.g. Jensen and Meckling, 1976). However, there have been concerns that this framework overemphasizes the negative aspects of self-interested behaviour where managers are portrayed as deceitful shirkers (e.g. Donaldson, 1990; Castanias and Helfat, 1991). If it exaggerates the supposed deceitfulness of managers, it has also remained silent about the ramifications of firms acting self-interestedly with regard to their managers and employees, preferring to leave this to the labour process debate (see Braverman, 1974). Castanias and Helfat (1991: 163) argue that:

> ... to the extent that managers can appropriate the quasi-rents associated with their skills, managers have disincentives to misbehave because job loss would result in the loss of firm-specific and perhaps even industry-related quasi-rents. Depending on a manager's mix of skills and the types of rents these skills generate, the opportunity to collect rents can provide positive incentives for efficiency rent generation as well as disincentives to misbehave.
>
> (Castanias and Helfat, 1991: 163)

Applying this logic to ordinary employees might suggest that individuals are not necessarily predisposed to act self-interestedly and that indeed the scope for opportunistic behaviour is lessened when they have sufficient scope to appropriate 'above-normal rates of return' and other intangibles. Such incentives might perhaps persuade individuals to align their activities more closely with the interests of the firm. This argument could be taken further to examine whether it is a more fruitful way to theorize work behaviour than current theories of motivation and commitment. We return to this point below.

Strategic management theorists like Grant see appropriation in terms of appropriating identifiable rents. If in the context of HRM the appropriation question were that straightforward, it would perhaps be resolved by existing frameworks within industrial relations and collective bargaining. However, appropriation should be viewed within a much broader context which takes into account people's interest in the organization; the nature of the knowledge they possess and how this knowledge comes to be constituted; the relevance, if any, of property rights over such knowledge; and the effect of technological advancement on the nature of work and the utilization of resources (KSAs). Ultimately what the debate requires is a more lucid articulation of an appropriation regime which is sociologically grounded.

Why appropriation?

The argument that individuals are concerned with appropriation is not new. As Kamoche and Mueller (1998) have argued, this can be explained with reference to a long-standing sociological question as to why people 'participate' in organizations. As such, in Weberian terms for example, whatever it is people are seeking from organizations, there is an understanding that the formally constituted system has sufficient legitimacy to govern the relationship, which for our purposes includes *inter alia* establishing rational mechanisms for generating and distributing rents. In such a scenario, individuals fully understand the nature of their contribution and potential outcomes, and will accept the appropriation regime to the extent that they recognize its legitimacy and are prepared to be bound by the terms of that regime.

Such a system does not depend merely on the rational decision making between the relevant stakeholders; it is also maintained by reciprocal trust. If workers have faith in the integrity of management, and trust management to make judicious decisions that are in the interest of workers, it can reasonably be assumed that the existing appropriation regime will remain stable. However, where doubts exist about the integrity of management, or where strategic decisions cast aspersions on such integrity perhaps by creating unexpected job insecurity or threatening careers, we can expect a realignment in the appropriation regime.

The quest for 'fit' and in particular the matching model of HRM provides only a nominal framework for addressing appropriation. By specifying how HR practices can be matched to strategies, this model proposes how resources will be deployed in what kinds of activities. The model does not suggest how resultant 'rents' will be distributed except with respect to matching remuneration policy to business strategy. An early depiction of the matching concept with regard to remuneration was made by Lawler (1984: 129) who stated that after the strategic plan is developed, the next step is to 'design reward systems that will motivate the right kind of performance, attract the right kind of people, and create a supportive climate and structure'.

Lawler concludes his discussion by suggesting that designing reward systems should be integrated within a human resource strategy 'that is consistent in the way it encourages people to behave, that attracts the kind of people that can support the business strategy, and *that encourages them to behave appropriately*' (1984: 147, emphasis added). Inherent in subsequent discussions within the notion of 'fit' is the view that the individual will be rewarded to the extent that he/she behaves *appropriately*, i.e. in line with the organizationally defined precepts which include performance standards. This is epitomized in performance-related pay. These processes further illustrate how strategic human resource management has been influenced by developments in strategic management.

Limits to appropriation

The effect of the above tradition has been to reinforce the organization's proprietorial claims over the KSAs that reside *within* the individual. As noted above, the organization is presumed to own or at least control the resources at its disposal. This is what allows managers to dispose of assets like money, equipment, raw materials, in whichever way they see fit. The discovery of the resource-based view by HRM writers runs the risk of extending the power 'to dispose' to the KSAs as well. Much of the existing RBV/SHRM literature has remained silent on the question of appropriation. This represents a selective reading of the RBV and an implicit acquiescence in the assumption that the firm's right to appropriate human resources is not in dispute. Adversarial labour relations throughout the history of industrialization show this to be wrong. According to Kamoche (1996a: 224), 'Rent appropriation by the firm cannot presuppose the institutionalization of human resources since organizations do not "own" people or (human resource competencies) in the same way they own patents or physical property.'

Thus the firm's hand in the appropriation exercise is constrained by a number of factors:

- uncertain ownership or possession of KSAs;
- undefined property rights over KSAs;
- the individual's capacity to negotiate;
- collective bargaining;
- the threat of industrial action;
- individual or collective mobility.

We consider these factors below.

For Grant (1991a: 128), appropriation is 'the allocation of rents where property rights are not fully defined'. Grant proceeds to identify two major problems in the area of 'employee skills'. The first one is the blurred distinction between the technology of the firm and the human capital of the individual. The second problem is the limited control employment contracts offer over the services employees provide.

As for the first point, the important question is: how much does the organization depend on the special skills of an individual and how are the individual's skills tied to the organizational routines? In sports, professional firms and high-tech firms, it is quite possible that one individual's knowledge, talents, contacts etc. are the prime source of success (or at least play a decisive role as part of a team effort), hence rents for the organization. This could be illustrated in the case of 'junk bond' pioneer Michael Milken at Drexel Burnham Lambert (before their collapse following alleged fraud), or the basketball star Michael Jordan at Chicago Bulls. The extent to which high-profile achievers can retain their autonomy in task performance limits the organization's appropriative ability while enhancing that of the individual.

This is evident in the individual's ability to negotiate astronomic rewards and other privileges that are beyond the reach of more *the RBV (?) assumption that firms own their employees is incorrect.*

ordinary performers. This might include liberties in time management; bending the rules to accommodate their idiosyncrasies; being let off lightly for breaches like missing important meetings or practice sessions, and so forth. There are of course limits to such liberties and organizations particularly in sports have been known to exercise their residual powers to protect their appropriative capacities by imposing severe penalties on wayward players.

As noted above, the modern organization does not *literally* own people. Such a notion belongs to feudal societies or slavery. In effect, the individual and organization have a mutual exchange relationship characterized by formal and psychological contracts (Schein, 1978; Robinson *et al.*, 1994; Rousseau, 1995; Grant, 1999). The individual continues to provide his/her labour/KSAs in exchange for specified or tacit rewards and benefits. In theory, therefore, the firm will appropriate benefits arising from the utilization of the individual's KSAs within the confines of the employment agreement, and to the extent that the individual permits it. Due to the tacit nature of the knowledge attributable to individuals, and the fact that organizations do not have a complete record of what the individuals are doing, even with the benefit of advanced surveillance mechanisms, it is possible therefore that the organization's appropriative scope may be subject to the individual's cooperation.

Cooperation here means a willingness to share knowledge and to work within the laid-down governance structure which allows the organizational objectives to be achieved in the most efficient way possible, and a willingness to allow the organization to benefit from one's knowledge. It is possible for the individual to withhold his/her labour through absenteeism, go-slows or strike action, or simply by quitting. The opportunity also exists for people to apply their KSAs to other activities and indeed other jobs thus potentially depriving their employer of the full benefits of their expertise. The use of technology has made it that much easier for people to engage in such activities on company time and with company assets. Surveillance techniques are not always effective in curtailing these activities. Furthermore, the fact that some organizations find it necessary to watch their staff reinforces our argument that claims to own or control human resources must be treated with suspicion.

The capacity to negotiate is one feature that clearly distinguishes between people (human capital) and other assets (e.g. machinery). Thus, while a machine's only *claim* on the organization is regular maintenance and upgrading – i.e. it is limited by the demands of depreciation – the individual has a wider range of claims, limited by real or perceived requirements and, ultimately, greed. The nature of wants, needs, requirements and so forth has been thoroughly explored within motivation theory and will not be rehearsed here. The question of what individuals want in return for their effort is a much more complex issue which extant discussions of 'reward management' are yet to exhaust.

Coff (1999) rightly points out that if the firm is indeed a 'bundle of resources' as suggested by the RBV, then we must define what holds the bundle together. This in turn implies that we must define the constituent actors who own or control the various resources. Drawing from Jensen and Meckling (1976), Coff treats the firm as a *nexus of contracts* – the various stakeholders are tied together by implicit contracts. The relationships between these stakeholders and the respective levels of bargaining power they can muster are factors that play a vital role in establishing who appropriates what. Bargaining power is highest when stakeholders can act in concert, have access to information, and when their departure involves high replacement costs to the firm and high personal costs of exiting (see Coff, 1999: 122).

Acting in concert is a basic principle in industrial relations which allows unions to increase their power relative to management. Some authors treat 'rent' as what accrues to employees over and above what is necessary to stop them from quitting (see for example Milgrom and Roberts, 1992). Defining the level of pay/benefits that would stop them from quitting is the domain of bargaining, whether at the individual or collective level. Professional employees and managers who are rarely unionized face a unique problem in their limited scope to act in concert.

In fact the increased move towards 'individualized arrangements' through merit pay (or performance-related pay) has further restricted such people from enjoying the protections available to workers in traditional trade unions. Staff associations do not generally enjoy the same amount of recognition, hence power and legitimacy, as traditional unions. Often, professionals and managers have to rely on their ability to bargain, and on the minimal protections provided under contracts of employment. However, when the internal protective mechanisms prove inadequate, aggrieved parties often have to resort to expensive litigation.

As the organizational power literature has demonstrated (e.g. Martin, 1977; Mintzberg, 1983; Pfeffer, 1992), access to and control of information – and knowledge – are important sources of power. In the 'information age' this issue becomes even more pertinent – the notion of causal ambiguity implies that where it is not obvious what particular factors are responsible for superior performance, the individual who *knows* enjoys special bargaining power. This explains why so much time and so many resources are expended to gather privileged information and, equally importantly, to act on it expeditiously. Just as organizations seek a competitive edge through their management of information and time, people also recognize the potential benefits of acquiring esoteric knowledge, be it some special problem-solving skill or company secrets on the politics of promotion. The effect is to enhance one's power relative to others or to the organization, which has important implications for the appropriative regime.

Organizations find themselves under pressure to control or curtail the use of such power by codifying knowledge and embedding it more closely within organizational routines. Alternatively, they try to achieve the same objective through firm-specific training – equipping people only with those skills that are crucial to the performance of their task and which would be largely useless to rival employers. The attractiveness of such an approach is that it is actually beneficial to those who have no particular intention of securing alternative employment and who want to enhance their career prospects internally.

It is also beneficial for those who are genuinely interested in improving their competencies at work irrespective of where they see themselves working in the future. The flip side of the coin is that the tacit nature of many KSAs suggests that codification of knowledge can be severely limited. This might explain the pre-occupation to codify practices instead; but it is meaningless to maintain control over highly codified practices in order to manage tacit and largely uncodifiable KSAs. In a similar vein, Mueller

(1996) notes that the practice of formalizing policies and rules within the informal context of organizations is highly questionable. In such circumstances, the employee can exercise residual control over the KSAs and, by implication, a relative advantage in appropriative capacity.

High costs may accrue to the organization in seeking to replace key performers who have quit. This has been recognized in the recruitment literature (see for example Heneman *et al.*, 2000). Replacement costs may be direct and easily measurable – e.g. the costs of placing advertisements and reimbursing travel costs to interviewees. Less obvious are those involving the interviewers' time, the loss of valued expertise and a possible decline in the morale of remaining staff. The notion of substitutability is relevant to this discussion. As the RBV suggests, a resource is valuable if it is inimitable or nonsubstitutable. The more difficult it is to replace an employee, the higher the overall replacement cost and the higher the employee's relative bargaining power. It should be noted that the exercise of switching jobs can also be costly to the individual – the individual will incur certain 'switching costs', i.e. transaction costs of mobility.

Though some monetary costs may be involved, the psychological ones are likely to be more significant. Readjusting to a new work environment, new region/country can involve a major disruption to one's way of life, and may be particularly stressful where a family is involved. The uncertainties of a new job, the loss of familiar surroundings, possible discouragement from friends, colleagues and family can all play a part in raising the stress component of the switching costs. The expatriate literature has demonstrated the difficulties people face in acclimatizing to a foreign environment (e.g. Tung, 1988; Forster, 1994; Selmer, 1999).

In fact, the stress involved, culture shock, loss of spouse's income, disruption of children's education, loss of vital contacts and so forth are factors that can combine to make a job change unattractive whether at the local or international level. The resultant switching costs can ultimately reduce the individual's relative bargaining power, thus reducing his/her appropriative capacity. Therefore, although the firm does not literally own the employee, it can exercise a high degree of control over the KSAs attributable to that employee if he/she faces high mobility costs.

We conclude this discussion with the following propositions (from the firm's point of view; the reverse applies to the employee): The firm's apropriative capacity is increased when:

- the employees' KSAs are embedded within the organizational routines, or are highly codified;
- the organization plays a dominant role in the definition and utilization of KSAs;
- the organization can substantially restrict 'outside' work;
- leavers can be replaced with relative ease;
- employees cannot act in concert in making and enforcing their demands;
- an employee's switching costs are relatively high.

By a similar token, an employee will have a relatively higher appropriative capacity if he/she has critical (and rare) skills, access to privileged information, high replacement costs and low switching costs.

Finding a role for retention

We suggest here that for an organization to develop an effective appropriation regime it is necessary to address the question of employee retention. Although we have identified the crucial role of generating KSAs and devising some mechanism for their deployment, it should be understood that the firm can only begin to appropriate rents from the utilization of KSAs if it is possible to retain key performers who are responsible for generating rent at least for a period of time. At its most basic, the argument is based on the view that dysfunctional turnover leads to knowledge spillover whereby a firm's investments in training and development are effectively 'harvested' by rival firms. This is evident in managers' reluctance to train when there is a real threat of people leaving and cashing in on their knowledge elsewhere. Closer to the academic's world, a retention failure by one university would mean that the new employer 'harvests' the researcher's publications come the next research assessment exercise.

The task of retention can be conceived of in terms of a firm's *human resource retention capacity* (HRRC). This can be thought of as consisting of the cumulative effects of human resource activities designed to attract and retain employees coupled with efforts to prevent dysfunctional turnover. The HRRC is closely tied in with the provision of a clear career path and career prospects which are attractive enough to persuade individuals to immobilize themselves and exhibit a sufficiently high level of behavioural commitment. To make sense of the HRRC construct we need to acknowledge the interactive nature of appropriation and retention: a retention capacity provides the initial scope for appropriation. Similarly, by giving employees an opportunity to appropriate some of the HR rents, the organization can strengthen its retention capacity. This recursiveness (cf. Giddens, 1976; Clark, 2000) illustrates the fact that the 'appropriation regime' does not have to be conceptualized as a zero-sum game, as implied by much of the existing literature on appropriation.

In his development of the conception of appropriation Coff (e.g. 1999) identifies the need 'for research exploring the structure of the "bargaining process"' to examine how stakeholders apply bargaining power. We reiterate this call here but modify it somewhat to propose that such a process might focus on the stakeholders' stated and implicit claims on rent; the way they define the interests underpinning their claims; the actual mechanism(s) of the rent distribution process; and the institution of conflict resolution mechanisms.

We suggest further that such a process in effect represents a contest over comparative discretion in the creation and utilization of KSAs. The contestants thus operate or manoeuvre across zones which intersect and overlap but which are also subject to divergent forces. Comparative discretion within these *zones of manoeuvre* (Kamoche and Cunha, 1999; cf. Clark, 2000) thus represents the scope available to achieve a comparative edge in the appropriation regime. This will necessarily involve trade-offs and compromises because of the ambiguous nature of KSAs and the even more uncertain nature of property rights over knowledge.

Lowenstein's (1997) *Wall Street Journal* report on rent distribution at Microsoft identifies an increasingly important area for rent distribution: stock options. This report details how the software giant has embraced and treated its knowledge-workers as an important stakeholder group by awarding them substantial bundles of stock options at far below market price. Such options effectively constitute a financial liability to the firm and, more importantly, serve as an appropriative tool for employees, who are in effect competing with the investors for rent. This tool also serves to secure retention in the medium to long term. In the next section we discuss in more detail how organizations effect retention and appropriation through barriers.

The role of resource and mobility barriers in appropriation

Resource and mobility barriers help to prevent the loss of value and to 'lock in' this value within the organizational routines. Within the HR debate, this refers to mechanisms to prevent the loss of valued employees in order better to appropriate their KSAs. It is useful to relate this argument to innovation management where the importance of resource barriers and the need to appropriate returns from innovative activities are well established. This is sometimes seen in terms of 'capturing' value (e.g. Teece, 1986), largely through a regime defined by patents, copyrights, legislation and other codifiable protective mechanisms. The problem of appropriating returns from innovation, however, has never been fully resolved.

Replicability and imitability are important notions in the RBV. Imitation and replication are, nevertheless, rampant, especially in the performing arts. For example, a Hong Kong daily, the *South China Morning Post*, reported that the International Federation of the Phonographic Industry estimates that the compact disc global pirate industry is about US$4.5 billion and rising (Tsang, 1999). Kay (1995) notes that the fear of replication reduces the incentive to innovate. Similarly, the fear of imitation and the absence of adequate protection over intellectual property rights can prevent organizations from investing in creative activities. The reluctance by large firms like Warner Brothers and EMI to invest in some parts of Asia, either in artist development or production facilities, is due partly to this fear of piracy.

In the field of manufacturing, 'reverse-engineering' is said to have played a pivotal role in the rejuvenation of Japanese industry

71

in the earlier days. Eiji Toyoda, a relative of the founder of the Japanese motor giant, Toyota, who also led the company for many years, recalls the turning point in his car-making career in their research laboratory. The founder of Toyota, Kiichiro Toyoda, had asked a Professor Kumabe to bring back 'any interesting cars' he found in the west. Eiji Toyoda reports:

> Kumabe bought a German front-wheel-drive called the DKW and shipped it over to us. After driving this around for a while, we took it apart, then proceeded to test-build several cars based on it. I handled drawings of the engine, while Ikenaga made drawings of the chassis and other parts. *It was the first time that drawings I made were transformed into a real car.* All told, we must have made about ten of them. These we drove, then took apart again to inspect and study some more.
>
> (Toyoda, 1987: 45, emphasis added)

Toyota currently holds 8 per cent of the world car market, while the market leader, General Motors has 12 per cent. The reality is that innovations are easily copied, whether they enjoy the protection of copyright, patents, or not. Protective structures like patents and copyrights can also be very expensive to procure and police. These measures may be woefully inadequate where a weak intellectual property protection regime exists; in such cases, firms may find it useful to rely on complementary assets (e.g. Teece, 1986; Tripsas, 1997).

Kogut (1991) argues that innovations in organizational and management practices diffuse more slowly than those in technology. These conclusions are drawn from a survey of the literature on how transfer practices are associated with competitive advantage. This finding implies that there is more scope to institute successful resource barriers in management practice, which for our purposes includes practices relating to the management of people. With reference to the innovation management literature, Kamoche and Mueller (1998) apply the notion of 'absorptive capacity' to explain a firm's capacity to acquire the knowledge that resides in the employees/managers and absorb it within the organizational routines. Cohen and Levinthal (1990) had earlier applied this concept to innovation management.

Within the domain of transaction cost economics, Williamson

(1987) has put forward the notion of a governance structure to prevent the loss of value of highly specific and non-transferable skills. At the practical level, such structures constitute retention mechanisms such as deferred compensation in the form of pensions, stock options, the synergies of teamwork, firm-specific skills, firm-specific routines and so forth (see also Williamson, 1975; Cappelli and Singh, 1992; Coff, 1997). These mechanisms act as resource and mobility barriers to the extent that they raise the employee's switching costs and make alternative jobs less desirable. They also reduce the transferability of the employee's KSAs. Within the internal labour market debate, such mechanisms also serve to explain the existence of long-term employment relationships (e.g. Siebert and Addison, 1991).

The success of such mechanisms cannot be guaranteed – there is always the possibility of poaching (Mueller, 1996) and people simply leaving unless they are physically prevented from doing so (as in the case of some sweatshops where workers are literally imprisoned on factory premises). As Coff (1997) puts it, as the firm's assets (i.e. people) walk away from the firm each day, there is always a question about whether they will return. It should be understood that resource and mobility barriers are a double-edged sword. As Cappelli and Singh (1992) have noted, reducing voluntary turnover can be a serious obstacle during organizational change when it becomes necessary to downsize or replace people. This in part explains the high severance costs associated with organizational restructuring, including early retirement packages and 'golden handshakes'.

In closing we note that the appropriation process essentially has to be a negotiated one – within discretionary zones of manoeuvre. It would be erroneous to assume that all employees in all cases are interested in rent appropriation. In periods of job insecurity and high unemployment, perhaps a vast number of people are happy just to have a job and are unconcerned about appropriating a portion of the 'above normal rates of return'. They may also be unaware that such rents exist and that they might be entitled to them. It is in this regard that Kamoche and Mueller's (1998) 'appropriation-learning' perspective offers a way forward. According to this perspective, there is a need to move away from some of the traditional approaches to managing people which are cast in a unitarist mode and which hardly treat the question of appropriation at all.

When they do, they invariably work with the assumption that the appropriation exercise is exclusively that of the firm. One example is training: emphasis should move away from mere skill formation to a concern with knowledge creation and associated mechanisms for determining the absorption and diffusion of learning. Employees do not just want to acquire skills; in fact they may be particularly averse to firm-specific skills except in the earlier stages of their career when they desperately need to know the ropes. Instead they may well want to see a specific learning trajectory that specifies the 'outcomes of the expertise attributable to themselves' (Kamoche and Mueller, 1998: 1047). They may also want an opportunity for personal development, job satisfaction, a congenial working environment, and fairness in the way they are treated. These issues go beyond the psychological contract and are in fact part of the broader appropriation regime – thus constituting a broader agenda for the management of people. In the following chapter, we consider in more detail how the emergent concepts of knowledge and learning fit into this debate.

6

KNOWLEDGE MANAGEMENT: AN EMERGENT PARADIGM

This chapter discusses the concept of knowledge and what it means for the management of people. The concept of knowledge became a buzzword in the late 1990s and appears clearly poised to take centre stage in management in the third millennium. The seeds of this phenomenon were sown in the earlier developments in data processing and the move toward automation. The debate ran alongside the stipulations of the emergence of a technocracy and the powerful role of knowledge in 'the post-industrial society' (e.g. Galbraith, 1967; Bell, 1973; Drucker, 1993). These authors and many others working in this genre recognized that the industrial workplace would gradually evolve around the possession of special skills and technical expertise. With the rolling back of manual labour through automation, attention inevitably shifted to the cognitive processes.

This theme has now been taken up more widely in the management debate by those who recognize that, increasingly, people will be valued for *what they know*, rather than what they do (e.g. Liu *et al.*, 1990). This again seems to represent a shift in emphasis away from brawn to brains. The technocracy has metamorphosed into knowledge-workers who work in knowledge-intensive firms (e.g. Starbuck, 1992; Alvesson, 1993) and is now increasingly embracing the Internet (Debrah, 1998). Attention is now being directed more specifically at the processes of creating and applying or utilizing knowledge (often conceptualized as expertise, talents, skills, abilities and so forth) to real organizational problems particularly through the management of innovation (see for example Nonaka and Takeuchi, 1995).

The knowledge management question is, however, more complex than that. As we noted in Chapter 5, knowledge connotes power, and issues related to power are of great importance to managers since they impinge on how the interests of the various stakeholders are mediated. Modern organizations based on sophisticated coordination systems have over time evolved mechanisms for maintaining and reproducing themselves (e.g. Reed, 1992). This has in turn brought to the surface the political/ideological concerns attendant on the use of knowledge particularly by 'professionals' or 'experts' (e.g. Dandeker, 1990; Bryant and Jarry, 1991). Thus, advances in technology have made it easier for organizations to install surveillance systems to monitor the activities of employees. We return to this point later.

There still remains a lot of confusion about the meaning of knowledge, and as Clark (2000) has recently observed, in many organizations there is no commonly held model for knowledge creation, embodiment and dissemination. There appears to be a strong emphasis on the production and utilization of knowledge which is now being perceived as a vital strategic asset. The argument is that if knowledge can be shown to be a valuable resource, it follows therefore that it must be applied to the improvement of organizational performance. This functionalist approach to the economics of knowledge management has been a seemingly logical development in the ongoing trajectory of strategic management, but as we argue in this chapter, it has left unanswered many concomitant questions about the socio-political context of the *production* of knowledge, and the role of people in the creation and utilization of knowledge.

In light of these debates, this chapter takes a critical look at the concept of knowledge and in particular the ways in which knowledge comes to be constituted in organizational reality. We highlight the contested nature of this constitution and the ways in which individuals strive to free themselves from structural and cultural control in order to exercise discretion in the application of the knowledge that is attributable to themselves. We develop the debate within the context of human resource management in order to examine as fully as possible the significance of the concept of knowledge in a field which deals directly with the creation and application of skills and competencies. There is still too much emphasis on so-called 'knowledge-workers', perhaps because the configuration of their skills in terms of knowledge is more readily visible. But human resource scholars should not restrict themselves to just one form of work or one category of workers. We need to go beyond these narrow confines and consider the implications of knowledge management in other areas of human endeavour.

The diversity of views about what constitutes knowledge reveals a more complex epistemological question – the status of knowledge itself: i.e. what is known and knowable, how society perceives and interprets the products of the human mind and, encompassing all these, how the process of knowing takes place. Scholars and management practitioners appear determined to eschew the earlier conception of knowledge within the narrower confines of information processing – how organizations generate and utilize data/information – and now increasingly recognize some of the wider implications, such as how to diffuse knowledge through innovative activities, aligning knowledge to organizational learning, and so forth. There is, clearly, a need to comprehend fully the implications of this form of pragmatism, from the utilitarian point of view of both the individual and the organization: how can both best use the knowledge for their own or joint interests? We argue here, however, that this must now be juxtaposed against a careful study of the epistemological, social and ideological dimensions of knowledge.

Therefore, the focus on the artefacts of knowledge (data, information, the mechanics of information processing, the products of processes such as inventions, patents etc.) should now shift to the *process* of knowledge creation and utilization (KCU). KCU involves generating capabilities for engaging in productive activities through the application of KSAs. This can also be illustrated by Starbuck's view that 'knowledge is a stock of expertise, not a flow of information' (1992: 716). Nonaka's seminal contribution (for example Nonaka, 1994) presents a model to examine the

Polanyi

'dynamic aspects' of knowledge creation processes. This model is based on the view that knowledge is created by the continuous dialogue between 'tacit' and 'explicit' knowledge.

The tacit–explicit dichotomy follows a long tradition going back to Polanyi (1962, 1967). Some of those working within the knowledge literature appear to have been locked into the tacit–explicit dichotomy from which they are unable to free themselves. We need to be aware that this is just one way of approaching the issue, and it should not preclude other formulations of knowledge. For example, following Boisot (1998), Clark (2000) proposes the notion of 'explacit' knowedge to move toward new analytical dimensions that combine tacit and explicit knowledge. Nonaka has built his entire theory of knowledge upon this tacit–explicit premise (see also Nonaka and Takeuchi, 1995). Adopting a definition of knowledge as 'justified true belief', Nonaka proceeds to define knowledge creation in terms of a tacit–explicit dialogue, hence:

- tacit to tacit: e.g. learning by observation in apprenticeships – socialization;
- explicit to explicit: bringing together, through social processes, different forms of information – combination;
- tacit to explicit: e.g. the conversion of tacit perspectives into explicit concepts – externalization;
- explicit to tacit: internalization of knowledge through 'learning by doing'.

For Nonaka, these processes exist within an unitarist world where middle managers are the 'knowledge engineers' who 'synthesize the tacit knowledge of both frontline employees and top management, make it explicit, and incorporate it into new technologies and products' (Nonaka, 1994: 32). It is suggested here that this unitarist dimension is one of the central weaknesses of Nonaka's theory. Nonaka argues that 'through the use of contradiction and paradox, dialectic can serve to stimulate creative thinking in the organization' (1994: 25). He does not, however, develop the full implications (social, political and ideological) of the concept of *dialectic* to explore the contested nature of knowledge creation, despite having recognized the existence of 'communities of interaction'. Spender (1996: 48) describes this positivist approach as a 'naïve neo-Kantian view' which assumes that tenable knowledge is the result of systematic analysis.

The unitarist orientation of Nonaka's work leads him away from the critical question: who owns or controls knowledge? His 'spiral' model is about how 'communities of interaction' amplify, share and develop knowledge, so that eventually 'concepts which are thought to be of value obtain a wider currency and become crystallized' (1994: 15). It may be inferred from his discussion of the practical management of the knowledge creation process that any questions relating to the 'ownership' of knowledge are resolved by the middle managers. This unitarist stance implicitly disregards the claims that other stakeholders might have to property rights because their interests are presumed to be consistent with the demands of the spiral, whose role is seen as the 'synergistic expansion of knowledge' (1994: 34). Thus, while Nonaka's conception of knowledge has no doubt contributed immensely to our understanding of the nature of knowledge, the debate now needs to go further and embrace the more problematic issues that define the social and political context of organizations. We now turn to these important dimensions in KCU with a view to clarifying the nature of their constitution and their implications for HRM.

Dynamism in the process of knowledge creation and utilization

The dynamic nature of knowledge implies that it is subject to constant change as it is generated, as it evolves over time and in the way it manifests itself. This dynamism is also evident in the interaction between the essence of knowledge itself and those involved in its generation and conception. Two important points arise from this: first, the constitution of knowledge presupposes a reason for this constitution. It is this which leads us to query the objectives behind the creation of knowledge. These may be hypothesized to be functionalist, economic, personal, social, political, ideological and so forth. The second point is about the use to which knowledge is put. This notion of utilization underpins the appropriation issue: who benefits from the use of knowledge, or how are the benefits distributed?

In explicating this issue, it can be assumed that the creators and users of knowledge are necessarily affected both by the processes of KCU and by its outcomes. This recursiveness has not been considered in Nonaka's model. For Nonaka, dynamism is manifested in the 'continuous interaction' between two forms of knowledge: tacit and explicit. Dynamism can also be conceptualized not just in terms of the relationships between alternative constitutive elements of knowledge, but in terms of the forces (and people) that bring this constitution about, and how the constitutive elements of knowledge in turn act back on its defining forces/people to alter the relationship further between the forces/people and knowledge.

In other words, not only are we shaping the nature of knowledge, it is also shaping us and leading to new relationships between us and the knowledge we create. Giddens (e.g. 1976) has developed this type of recursiveness in his theory of structuration to demonstrate for example how people's actions, i.e. social outcomes, are at the same time operating as the medium through which the outcomes become possible. The dynamic nature of knowledge creation is sometimes thought of as *knowing*. For example, Blackler (1995) has advanced the notion of knowing by drawing from 'activity theory', to highlight 'the processes through which people develop shared conceptions of their activities' (1995: 1035) and how communities enact these conceptions. We develop this theme further in the sections that follow.

The social construction of knowledge

What constitutes knowledge is generally a matter for the social actors or relevant stakeholders. The stakeholder notion is particularly important because it points to the existence of interests, some of which may be congruent, and others diametrically opposed. These may ultimately be defined or resolved through processes of negotiation. People working in a particular discipline shape the direction and content of knowledge through their practices and language. This social dimension is widely acknowledged. It became widely accessible to management theory through Berger and Luckmann's seminal work (1966). Nonaka (1994) recognizes this dimension in his 'communities of interaction'. Similarly, within the context of activity theory, Blackler (1995) talks about 'communities of practitioners'. In defining his concept of a 'paradigm', Kuhn (1962) offers the term 'disciplinary matrix' to denote the common possession of the practitioners of a particular discipline; 'matrix' denotes the 'ordered elements' of various sorts and indicates how the community is structured. It is this conception of the paradigm that Masterman (1970) categorizes as the 'sociological paradigm', as distinct from the 'metaphysical paradigm or metaparadigm' (a *weltanschauung* which is ideologically prior to theory) and the 'artefact or construct paradigm' (a more 'concrete' conception more directly related to problem solving). The emphasis for these various observers is the social context, which for our purposes is critical to knowledge creation.

The notion of a paradigm seems like an appropriate metaphor for the evolution of knowledge. In this regard, Kuhn observes that progress takes place within a tradition of 'normal science', which he describes as 'research firmly based upon one or more past achievements, achievements that some particular scientific community acknowledges for a time as supplying the foundation for its further practice' (1962: 10). The evolution of a paradigm denotes the process of KCU by a community of practitioners. It is the problematic nature of this process that this chapter is concerned with, particularly as it relates to the management of people. As we noted in previous chapters, the unitarism inherent in strategic HRM grossly misrepresents the reality of social relations in the organizational context. Within the context of the appropriation debate, it can reasonably be assumed that knowledge is created within a contested social milieu (see also Alvesson, 1993; Knights *et al.*, 1993; Blackler, 1995). The contested nature of KCU arises from potential disagreements about what constitutes knowledge, how it should be created, and by whom, what use(s) it should be put to, and who appropriates it. By locating KCU within a dynamic social context the diversity of interests of the stakeholders within the 'knowledge community' begins to unravel.

For our purposes here, therefore, this diversity is mediated by processes of negotiation and compromise as the stakeholders struggle to reach consensus on how to generate, utilize and appropriate KSAs. The arenas within which these contests are played out include collective bargaining; performance appraisals for wage determination and promotion; management by objectives; the processes of employee selection and deployment and the dynamics of career development. These activities are part of an extensive process of labour regulation and control. With the emergence of modern human resource management in the 1980s with an emphasis on productivity, flexibility, merit rewards and so forth, and the subsequent erosion of job security and the redefinition of organizational commitment, the social context in the workplace has witnessed a heightened sense of politicization. What constitutes viable expertise is no longer defined solely from the organization's point of view; it has, in fact, assumed greater importance to individuals who increasingly find themselves concerned with their long-term *employability* – the capacity to secure employment in the event of downsizing and similar employment rationalization strategies. What does this all mean to HRM? This analysis has yielded new insights into the contested nature of the social context within which organizations manage people.

Is knowledge self-perpetuating?

The social dimension of KCU is further evident in the methods of self-perpetuation and exclusivity to which members of 'knowledge communities' often resort. Knowledge-intensive firms (Starbuck, 1992) learn by 'managing training and personnel turnover, and by creating physical capital, routines, organizational culture, and social capital' (1992: 715). Starbuck further notes that professional groups create high thresholds for membership. This is supposed to impose some discipline in knowledge creation by clarifying the requisite qualifications and training, and to uphold quality both in membership and the service(s) they offer. It also serves to enhance the visibility and status of the members, and to legitimate their claims to expertise.

We illustrate this with reference to the legal profession. Not only does the lengthy training of lawyers restrict entry into the profession; being 'called to the bar' in the case of barristers denotes entry into an exclusive community of high-status, high-income social actors. Hence, those in the legal profession – barristers, solicitors and judges – can, on the basis of their claims to a unique expertise which they themselves have created, subsequently proceed to define what constitutes acceptable legal practice, hence legal knowledge. The same principle can be applied, with variations, to any other profession or craft, from academia, medical practice or carpentry to stand-up comedy. This falls within the sociology of the professions (e.g. Elliot, 1972; Watson, 1989) and for our purposes can also be conceptualized as *the political manoeuvres involved in the social construction of esoteric knowledge.*

This argument has important implications for HRM, particularly in the case of so-called 'knowledge-workers'. It has a bearing, for example, on the extent to which the community of practitioners enjoy autonomy to shape the essence and destiny of their profession or craft, i.e. to what extent people, working collectively, can determine what constitutes a stock of expertise (i.e. KSAs). Professionals, acting in their own individual or collective interests, are often well placed to make such decisions because of the institutional mechanisms they have put in place for determining 'membership'. Such mechanisms include long training periods; selectivity through a process of restricting entry to a privileged cadre such as scientific and professional associations; peer assessment; entry through secret procedures, and so forth. It is natural for such groupings to guard their membership jealously and also, in many cases, to resist change, especially where that change is imposed from outside through legislative or regulatory authorities.

Debates about whether the media should come under regulatory Press Councils, whether complaints against the police should be investigated by independent parties and so forth, are illustrative in this regard. Resistance to external pressure, control over membership and the quest for more power to act in their own interests are examples of how knowledge can be turned into a self-perpetuating phenomenon. Knowledge can also be perpetuated by the concept of 'absorptive capacity' (Cohen and Levinthal, 1990) whereby prior knowledge creates a capacity, for example through learning abilities, to acquire and assimilate new knowledge.

Dierickx and Cool's (1989) concepts of 'time compression diseconomies' and 'asset mass economies' may help to clarify this further. The former refers to the cumulative value of advantages that can arise from a history of previous investments, while the latter says that the possession of initial high levels of an asset stock facilitates further accumulation of that asset. Thus, firms which possess high levels of some specific knowledge (including human resources) are likely to enjoy a comparative advantage in attracting or otherwise securing more of the critical resource. This leads us to the view that firms with a reputation for investing in people, or achieving high returns, may be well placed to attract high performers, thus allowing success to feed on success.

Is knowledge context-specific?

We now turn our attention to the context-specificity of knowledge and look at how this impacts on labour regulation. Due to the dynamic nature of knowledge, what constitutes knowledge even within a 'knowledge community' will change from time to time. New and more efficient technologies replace inefficient ones which can no longer be thought of as part of the knowledge base. This is because what constitutes knowledge has much to do with what the community and other stakeholders actually believe to be *valuable*. In a similar vein, Starbuck (1992: 722) suggests that 'for old knowledge to have meaning, people must relate it to their current problems and activities', and 'for new knowledge to have meaning, people must fit it into their current beliefs and perspectives'.

The use of punch cards in computers was once part of the knowledge base in computer technology; this is no longer the case. Laws that have outlived their usefulness are often repealed. Modern medicine and clinical procedures have now superseded magic in treating illnesses. Context-specificity in these kinds of cases is predicated upon considerations like timeliness, functionality and effectiveness. By a similar token, ideas which have not yet been realized can only be treated as frontiers of a potential knowledge base, such as the experience of human planetary landings.

Context-specificity can also be perceived in terms of disciplines. In the creation of 'academic knowledge', specificity manifests itself in the ways in which journal editors, reviewers and readers collaborate (some might say collude) to define and institutionalize both the nature of academic knowledge and the methods of its constitution which are acceptable to that particular community.

Consider church

The contested nature of this process is evident in the definition or interpretation of underlying assumptions which might lead reviewers to different conclusions. Locating this argument within the field of organization studies, it may be argued that organizational members are in a constant process of defining an organizational reality that is acceptable to themselves, either at the individual or collective level. The context-specificity of knowledge implies that the community of practitioners' view about what constitutes valuable knowledge may be at variance with those of other communities. This echoes Kuhn's postulation about the way scientists come to define their problematic, the tools for solving problems and the way progress is signalled by the emergence of new problems and new tools.

There is therefore a constant process of negotiation as to the validity of existing tools for problem solving. This is evident for example in the resistance that often meets new concepts that challenge conventional wisdom in academic research, or resistance to new technology, especially if it is perceived as threatening the status quo (including jobs). From the foregoing, we can argue therefore that social actors who have a vested interest in maintaining the status quo may be expected to protect their turf by resisting attempts by perceived outsiders to define for them the reality of their work. By so doing, they are indirectly enhancing the context-specificity of the knowledge attributable to themselves. Organizations attempt to deal with this issue by encoding knowledge and thus reducing their reliance on tacit knowledge and reducing the scope of individual discretion and manoeuvrability, such as by institutionalizing teamwork, where no one particular individual possesses a disproportionate amount of control over the organizational routines. This in effect helps to achieve some degree of regulation on people's behaviour and mobility, thus giving the organization a sense of stability. Below, we consider how this creates a paradox.

The paradox of control and discretion

Allowing people to exercise discretion over their KSAs inevitably raises the question of how organizational control might be

85

achieved to ensure that this discretion is not exercised self-interestedly. This problem is perhaps more acute in the case of 'knowledge-workers' whose day-to-day activities are notoriously difficult to monitor and where management may permit them a high degree of autonomy providing they deliver the goods. The effect of managerial control cannot be taken for granted. It cannot be assumed that discretion and control are necessarily diametrically opposed. The most visible manifestations are those whereby a tight control regime triggers resistance and such other responses as work-to-rule, restriction of effort and, in extreme situations, sabotage. On the other hand, empowerment and a participative and considerate management style might in fact elicit voluntary effort and commitment.

As we argued above, technological developments have led to an upsurge in the use of sophisticated control mechanisms. A typical example is the use of surveillance. The interesting thing here is not just how new forms of knowledge, i.e. technology, have facilitated the scope and intensity of control but how that knowledge is ultimately used against those who may have participated in its creation. This relates in particular to the use of highly advanced surveillance mechanisms – closed-circuit TV, tracking website visits etc. Such mechanisms are not merely used to watch for *organizational misbehaviour* including pilferage and disposing of trade secrets, but also to ensure employees are complying with corporate values like customer service, including smiling at customers.

While watching over staff may have some positive outcomes, the downside is found in the vast amount of pressure it places on those who have to deal with irate and unpleasant customers while retaining the prescribed smiling face. For example, Ogbonna (1992) identifies the contradiction whereby management in a supermarket appear intent on creating a culture of high trust and commitment but at the same time depend on high levels of surveillance to observe the behaviour of checkout operators. The operators sought solace by 'making rude remarks' about difficult customers privately.

People respond to organizational control in different ways, ranging from cynicism and recalcitrance to compliance. These forms of behaviour signal how people attempt to free themselves from the insidiousness of organizational control. Some theorists have proposed various approaches to modifying the nature of work as a response to managerial control or in order to circumvent the debilitating effects of managerial efforts to shape the organizational knowledge base and social relations. Anthony (1977) argues that if the obfuscations of ideology can be removed from work, it may be restored to its original virtues, by directing it at the production of good and useful objects and at meeting important needs. This will entail changing the setting, rather than merely the content, of the work. Meakin (1976) proposes a blurring of the distinction between work and art. Pym (1979) highlights the 'resourcefulness' of people which he says exists in people's inclination to work but often tends to be stifled by traditional forms of 'employment'. This notion of resourcefulness is developed further in Kamoche (1996b) who proposes a move away from the static nature of 'resource' to an acknowledgement 'of the proactive and voluntarist nature of human action which, at the organizational level is reflected in individual choice, innovativeness and a capacity to create' (1996b: 438). Organizational structures which allow for this resourcefulness have the potential to 'free' people from the more traditional employment practices that are built on bureaucratic control.

The emancipatory theme can be traced much farther back, for example to Habermas's (e.g. 1972) critical theory. Habermas offers an approach to examine how the forces of control and domination in language might be resolved in his 'symbolic interaction'. This subsequently allows us to understand how consensus as to what constitutes knowledge might be arrived at not through 'communication distortion' but through the 'ideal speech situation'. The challenge for managers is to manage the resourcefulness that exists within people while at the same time specifying some limits within which resourcefulness is exercised. Traditionally these limits have been defined unilaterally and without sufficient attention to the individual's residual discretion which might be applied against organizational interests. In the new millennium, it will become increasingly difficult for managers to rely on their institutional control mechanisms and on the expectation that the loyalty of employees can always be counted upon.

Notions like partnership and a more pluralistic mentality might help. But a fundamental problem still remains: how can management ensure that discretion is used 'responsibly', i.e. in line with organizational strategic objectives? In allowing a high degree of discretion, what assurances do managers have that people will apply their stock of knowledge in a manner consistent with organizational requirements rather than self-interestedly? Conversely, what assurances do people have that the knowledge and creativity they bring to the organization will not ultimately lead to their own redundancy? Underpinning this dilemma is the matter of choices and decision processes. On what basis do individuals make choices about the relative commitments they are faced with, and what *real* choices actually exist in terms of employment and knowledge-creation opportunities?

Technological advancement no doubt enhances these opportunities but, as we have argued above, it also offers new methods to institute or tighten organizational control. It is evident, therefore, that the control–discretion battle will be fought increasingly in the technological arena where new interpretations of the concept of knowledge are being thrown up every day, and where the zones of individual and organizational discretion are being redrawn. What this implies for managers is that they are not merely managing people, but the complex knowledge these people possess. As a result, the traditional control mechanisms are no longer appropriate and will need to be renegotiated.

Knowledge management and the RBV

Having discussed at length the various strands that constitute the knowledge debate, this section considers whether the concept of knowledge brings us any closer to understanding the full implications of the resource-based view of the firm for HRM. This issue is important in light of recent developments in the knowledge management literature where some writers are offering the 'knowledge-based view of the firm' (KBV) as a new analytical paradigm, or a new theory of the firm. Grant (1996: 109) correctly recognizes that there is no 'single, multipurpose theory of the firm', and that each theory is merely an abstraction of the real-world business environment. Theories thus act like lenses upon which to gaze and try to understand the 'real world'. In this sense, therefore, there is no reason why the knowledge-based view of the firm should not stake its claim alongside the myriad other perspectives that theorists have put forward to understand the world, such as transaction cost economics, the behavioural theory of the firm, the evolutionary theory, and so forth.

On closer scrutiny, however, it becomes apparent that the similarities between the KBV and the RBV are such that the two perspectives cannot really be analysed in isolation. Grant (1996: 110) recognizes that 'to the extent that it focuses upon knowledge as the most strategically important of the firm's resources, it is an outgrowth of the resource-based view'. The important link between the two perspectives is their concern with knowledge that resides in the first instance with individuals – this is the resource of knowledge. As many observers have noted, organizations learn because individuals do (e.g. Kanter, 1990; Argyris, 1993). Therefore, knowledge is first generated by people working with skills, abilities and talents that exist within them, and is then transferred to the organization. The managerial challenge with regard to securing organizational control is to ensure that mechanisms exist for this transfer to take place.

Such mechanisms include organizational learning, socialization, reward management and team working. In addition to ensuring knowledge transfer, they also serve to limit the organization's dependence on any one particular individual. This challenge lies at the heart of human resource management practices that seek to ensure that people are utilizing their skills towards the achievement of the organization's strategies. The KBV serves to redirect attention to the centrality of knowledge in these organizational activities, more specifically what we describe as KSAs.

The task for managers concerned with knowledge management is made more acute by the fact that much of the knowledge is *tacit*, which makes it difficult both to articulate and to codify and transfer. It is difficult and costly to transfer tacit knowledge which is observable through its application and cannot be sufficiently codified (Kogut and Zander, 1992). The significance of tacit knowledge has largely been associated with the work of Polanyi who identified the difficulty associated with apprehending knowledge that cannot be expressed in words. Since the tacit component of what we know is potentially so vast (it is associated with *experience*, in Polanyi's conceptualization), it follows that knowledge is of critical importance in view of the 'conditions' and definitive elements of the RBV such as inimitability and causal ambiguity.

According to Lippman and Rumelt (1982), uncertainty about what exactly leads to superior performance constitutes a source of competitive advantage. Similarly, Spender (1996: 46) has argued that 'competitive advantage is more likely to arise from the intangible firm-specific knowledge'. Even though it is the accumulated collective knowledge of organizational members that is ultimately reflected in organizational performance, the role of the individual remains critical to the process of knowledge creation and utilization. To the extent that the individual is the repository of this knowledge, the realms of the individual's KSAs become an important contributor to organizational performance which the individual may decide not to give willingly and fully so long as appropriation remains a moot point.

Knowledge and learning: some final thoughts

We conclude this chapter by considering what this concept of knowledge implies for HRM within the context of the learning organization. Nonaka and Takeuchi (1995) contend that Japanese firms learn by a continuous process of seeking new knowledge from outside, by turning to their suppliers, customers, distributors and so forth for new clues. They proceed to argue that 'knowledge that is accumulated from the outside is shared widely within the organization, stored as part of the company's knowledge base, and utilized by those engaged in developing new technologies and products' (1995: 6). This very broad approach to knowledge management has some useful lessons for organizations that do not currently foster continuous learning.

Senge's (1990) seminal work on learning offers some useful lessons for managers with regard to the creation of an environment in which organizational learning can take place. He suggests that managers should, inter alia, critically evaluate their own 'mental models' through which they understand the way the world works.

By so doing they enable people to have the confidence and ability to think and learn.

Whether a learning organization is really tenable is debatable, given the existing structural arrangements which preclude vital aspects of learning such as information sharing. Some observers suggest that the notion of a learning organization which facilitates the learning of all the organizational members and thus continuously transforms itself should be considered an ideal to aspire to, or a dream (see for example Pedler *et al.*, 1991). This is because it is difficult to realize the conditions for a scenario in which the managers actively create a climate of continuous critical thinking and reappraisal, where all employees accept the challenges of self-development and where mechanisms have been put in place to facilitate constant probing, experimentation and the sharing of knowledge.

In any case, it is unlikely that everything people learn is transferable or even beneficial to the organization. Similarly, individuals (including managers) may be reluctant or unable to transfer their learning to the organization for all kinds of reasons, some of which we have explored under the framework of appropriation. Also, Clark (2000) notes that developments in Penrosian learning have not been bold enough: the analysis needs to be related more to corporate action, organizational politics and Schumpeterian notions of creative destruction. What this discussion has hopefully clarified is the need to appreciate the problematic and political context in which people are involved in the process of generating a stock of expertise which the organization wants to apply to its productive activities.

7

INTERNATIONAL HRM

In the previous chapters we have assessed an array of human resource issues to enhance our appreciation of the critical formative debates. This chapter now locates the discussion within the international context. International HRM (IHRM) raises some very interesting questions about the employer–employee relationship especially in this era of globalization. We consider some important contemporary strands in this debate, the rationale underpinning the growth in interest in this area, the impact of globalization on HRM, and the significance and implications of appropriation within the global context. In this discussion we also take a look at the special case of the developing world which has tended to be ignored in the IHRM debate except to the extent that it constitutes a challenging destination for western expatriates.

It is almost *de rigueur* for writers on IHRM to begin their papers by remarking on the common weaknesses in the field as it has evolved from the late 1980s. In actual fact, this is hardly unusual in scholarly research in general. What is remarkable in IHRM is that despite these well-known weaknesses, there is not much evidence that scholars have begun to redress these shortcomings in a meaningful way. International HRM thus runs the risk of developing as a parochial subdiscipline alongside the more established

Weaknesses of IHRM research

debates in the mainstream HRM literature. Let us now place these weaknesses in perspective.

In a review of 338 papers published between 1977 and 1997, Clark *et al.* (1999) identify two major weaknesses in the comparative and IHRM research. The first one is the apparent 'insulation' from previous work and critiques of cross-national and international management research. As such, it appears that IHRM research has marked a territory for itself almost completely oblivious of critical debates in relevant related disciplines. These include debates on culture and the work on cross-cultural methodology from an anthropological perspective (e.g. Chapman, 1996), the socio-political context and the role of power. The second 'parochialism' Clark *et al.* identify is the Anglo-Saxon nature of much of the research. They argue that we need to move away from the parochialism inherent within Anglo-American research towards a more plural perspective.

These criticisms echo similar ones made almost a decade ago by Kochan *et al.* (1992) who identified the following limitations: a narrow focus on giving advice to firms on how to select and manage expatriates; a concern with the needs of international firms with little attention to theory; a predominance of American firms coupled with a neglect of the broader international context; and an overwhelming preference for cultural explanations as opposed to institutional, political, economic and strategic ones.

Many of these approaches and preferences can be explained by the fact that much of the literature has been about American firms and the challenges they face abroad (see also Kobrin, 1988; Boyacigiller and Adler, 1991; Scullion, 1995). Whether the impetus for an increased concern with the international context arose from the challenge of globalization and the need to enter or expand foreign markets, the threat from Asian economies, or the high domestic costs of production and so forth, one common response appears to have been triggered: how will the needs of American firms be met in these new competitive landscapes? What problems do these new, unfamiliar scenarios pose for American firms and American managers? Another point that no doubt fuelled interest in the above elements of international HRM was the discovery that American managers made bad expatriates abroad.

A number of alarming findings clearly showed that 'expatriate failure rates' were much higher for American than their Japanese and European counterparts (e.g. Tung, 1987). Subsequent research suggests that expatriates have made substantial progress in adopting a more cosmopolitan outlook (Tung, 1998). It appeared from previous research that European and Japanese managers were better at international adaptability, or at least were more prepared to see through their assignments in spite of the difficulties they encountered. Almost inevitably, the American response was to re-evaluate the selection practices for expatriates and to design new HR policies that would ensure only the most suitable candidates were selected for international assignments. Associated with this was a concern with training and rewarding; and these three HR areas have been the most important ones in the management of international assignees and expatriates (see also Mendenhall *et al.*, 1987; Tung, 1987; Scullion, 1993). Language/communication issues have recently begun to attract attention (e.g. Marschan-Piekkari *et al.*, 1999).

The training responsibility has thus embraced language training and cross-cultural awareness to develop a sensitivity to foreign cultures, while rewarding examines ways of designing remuneration packages that include sufficient incentives to take on difficult assignments in unfamiliar and in some cases hostile territories, compensation for hardships, managing tax in different jurisdictions etc. (see for example Dowling *et al.*, 1999). In the less well developed area of performance appraisal, attention has evolved around devising suitable criteria for evaluating performance given varying levels of difficulty, and how to achieve comparability where performance measures may be distorted heavily by economic and infrastructural conditions particularly in developing countries (e.g. Garland and Farmer, 1986).

Previously it was assumed, not just in American but in multinational firms in general, that success at the domestic level could translate into success in the international arena, i.e., managers who had demonstrated their mettle locally could be expected to replicate their competent performance anywhere. This is now recognized to be unrealistic. It should also be recalled that an 'international experience' has not always been considered useful from a career development point of view. From Japan to America, managers in the past tended to view an international assignment as a backward move which, apart from removing them from the fast-paced action and decision-making settings of the head office, was also, in many cases, not valued when career decisions were made. Returnees thus found little scope for advancement, and in some cases no real job. As a result, international assignees would either be the high performers who are compelled to accept the assignment, or average performers who are available and prepared to take the risk.

The literature on comparative management has largely rejected the universalist assumptions which fostered the belief that managers could apply certain sets of diagnostic and problem-solving tools and expect fairly similar results. In spite of all the claims made for the convergence of consumer behaviour in response to 'global brands', the world markets continue to be characterized by uniqueness borne of cultural–historical, technological and political–economic realities at the national and regional levels. The very notion that there are managers who can function effectively in any setting is thus rendered highly problematic. This in turn raises doubts about the approaches firms have adopted to develop managers for international assignments. Below we take a critical look at the issues that define management at the global level.

Managing firms at the global level

The internationalization of business particularly in the 1980s served as a strong impetus for the IHRM debate. A useful forum for this debate is journals like the *International Journal of Human Resource Management*. As organizations came face to face with the unprecedented complexities of doing business in unfamiliar territories, the question of how to manage their staff, and in particular their managers, on international assignments assumed more prominence. A number of conceptual frameworks have been put forward to explain the behaviour of multinational enterprises and the impact on human resources and managerial expertise (e.g. Bartlett and Ghoshal, 1989; Hendry, 1994; Dowling *et al.*, 1999).

Given the nature of global investments, one of the most important questions in the international management debates is how parent–subsidiary relationships are structured and in particular how subsidiaries in far-flung regions can best be integrated within the corporate structure. In a simple parent–single subsidiary model, keeping the subsidiary within the corporate fold may not present as tough a challenge as in the multiple subsidiary model with operations scattered across the globe.

An obvious question is how the centre maintains coordination and *control* over such subsidiaries. International management theorists have relied heavily on the resource-dependence concept to address this question (e.g. Pfeffer and Salancik, 1978). They argue that control and influence are tenable to the extent that the subsidiaries/affiliates are dependent on the parent for resources (e.g. Hedlund, 1981). This quasi-biological assumption thus allows the parent to nurture and, in return, to expect loyalty (and more importantly, value added) from the corporate children. For this model to operate effectively, it must be assumed that the managers of the subsidiary firms will work in the interest of the corporate centre. However, since this cannot be guaranteed where factors like geography render more direct forms of control untenable, other mechanisms must be found. These include the careful deployment of personnel, specifically placing senior managers in key top positions.

Human resource practices thus provide a potentially effective mechanism for instituting *appropriative control* over subsidiaries and affiliates. Central to the resource-dependence approach is the provision and use of resources, which implies that this approach cannot fully explain how this dependence relationship changes when the subsidiary is no longer heavily dependent on the parent for corporate nourishment. We would expect a relatively lower degree of local autonomy in the initial set-up stages, and as the subsidiary matures and establishes effective linkages with its respective environment, local managers may be allowed increasing levels of autonomy in decision making. The reality, however, is that due to the multifaceted nature of corporate control, autonomy is limited to certain low-level decisions while financial control remains firmly in the hands of the corporate centre.

Adopting an organizational life-cycle model, some authors have suggested that the internationalization process should be viewed as a series of sequential stages: domestic, international,

[handwritten: International firm v. multinational company]

multinational and global, or a variation on export, sales subsidiary, international division and global (e.g. Adler and Ghadar,
1990; Milliman *et al.*, 1991; Dowling *et al.*, 1999). The international
firm operates predominantly at the domestic level, with the business strategy centralized at the headquarters; its international
operations are treated as an adjunct to the main business strategy,
and are usually managed in a separate 'international division'.
The multinational firm operates across borders with its operations
treated as separate entities in need of integration by the headquarters. The global firm recognizes its worldwide operations as
an integral part of its business strategy; it therefore seeks to lever-
age its resources and technology globally, disregarding geo-
graphic constraints. For the sake of argument, we use the more
commonly acknowledged term 'multinational' to refer to all
multinational enterprises in general, except where there is a need
for more specific clarification.

Adler and Ghadar derive their model from product characteristics; hence product orientation, market orientation, price orientation and accelerated product life cycle. According to this school
of thought, the task for managers is to match human resource
strategies to the prevailing phase. This approach is thus consistent
with the concept of strategic fit and the situational–contingency
rationale.

The need to strike a balance between autonomy and control has
engendered a more sophisticated perspective which seeks to meet
the corporate centre's demands for integration while at the same
time facilitating flexibility and autonomy at the subsidiary level
(e.g. Bartlett and Ghoshal, 1989: Rosenzweig and Singh, 1991).
Bartlett and Ghoshal have claimed that firms which are able to
achieve this balance constitute a new organizational form: the
transnational. They include firms like Unilever and Philips. The
transnational would appear to be a more refined variant of the
global firm. The integration–differentiation dilemma in international management (Kamoche, 1996c) is more commonly
known as how to 'think globally and act locally'.

Whatever models we choose to work with, or however we
choose to conceptualize the dynamics of the internationalization
process, one key question remains: how does HRM fit into all this?
Above we mentioned how organizations use HR as a tool of

coordination and control. We examine below some of the other issues which researchers have been concerned with.

The human resource dimension

A number of loosely connected themes have come to be lumped together under the generic term 'international'. These include specific country studies; cross-national comparisons; the treatment of HR in joint ventures and other strategic alliances; the use of tools like selection, rewarding, training, and so forth. The area of training offers the opportunity to delve beyond the more typical treatment of skill formation and cross-cultural awareness and embrace the question of learning, knowledge creation and utilization. This is discussed in more detail below.

As noted earlier, competitive pressures forced multinational firms to tackle human resource issues that had previously not been considered an integral part of decision making in international management. Worries about 'expatriate failure' have played a pivotal role in this transformation. What we have seen as a result is a surfeit of articles devoted to the problems faced by expatriates and prescriptions as to how to solve these problems. Examples include the problems of British expatriates and the difficulties they face upon return – repatriation – (for example Forster, 1994), the problems faced by western expatriates in Asia (e.g. Aryee and Stone, 1996; Selmer, 1999), Japanese expatriates in Asia (Fukuda and Chu, 1994), and so forth. Also within this general field, Mamman and Richards (1996) have examined expatriates' perceptions of the relevance of their 'sociobiological' characteristics and backgrounds to their intercultural and cultural adjustment. Welch and Welch (1997) have called for a more systematic treatment of HR issues in these processes.

The idea of adjusting to harsh and perhaps hostile cultural environments appears to generate a lot of interest in the expatriate literature. Culture shock is undoubtedly a major problem that many expatriates face abroad as the voluminous literature shows. Similarly, many face difficulties in readjusting to an unfamiliar home setting after they have been away – the 'reverse culture shock' (Harvey, 1982). This is partly due to the unfamiliarity that results from a long absence and the fact that many organizations do not have well-established mechanisms and programmes to help repatriates readjust (e.g. Adler, 1986).

However, research in IHRM must go beyond this social well-being and adaptation agenda and begin to consider other equally relevant questions, for example the management of local personnel; interaction between local and expatriate personnel; the contribution of the KSAs to corporate performance through the effective leveraging of knowledge across the firm, and the scope for appropriation in these activities. Bartlett and Ghoshal's (1989) analysis focuses primarily on the leveraging of managerial expertise. The heavy emphasis on expatriate personnel has inevitably sidelined the situation of local personnel. So, while a lot is known about the selection, rewarding, training and adjustment of western and Japanese expatriates in foreign lands, there has been precious little research into the problems faced by 'host-country nationals' in multinational firms. Jain *et al.* (1998) note that much of the literature in this genre focuses on how firms adapt HRM practices to local conditions.

Anecdotal evidence suggests that problems exist on a wide scale: conflicts about wage inequalities whereby expatriates are perceived as overpaid; lack of training or promotion opportunities; accusations of arrogance on the part of expatriates; communication problems; cultural misunderstandings, and so forth. Perceptions of fair play and justice (both procedural and distributive) in the determination of wages of locals *vis-à-vis* those of expatriates has generated interest in some quarters, such as Leung *et al.*'s (1996) analysis of joint ventures in China. The domestic–expatriate staff interface is clearly a contested one, and one which calls for more empirical research in order to minimize or eliminate the scope for misconceptions. For example, it may be that what local staff consider 'arrogance' on the part of expatriates is in part due to the failure on all parties concerned to discern subtle cultural differences.

On the other hand, it is possible that expatriates from more developed economies might approach their staff in developing countries with an attitude that reflects the superiority of their lifestyle or workplace practices and technology. Consequently this might prevent them from appreciating new opportunities to learn from their local subordinates/managers. Also, Leung *et al.* (1996) suggest that managers in joint ventures should use decision-making processes that are consultative, open and responsive to feedback, and that they should communicate more with locals, explaining their pay scales in relation to other joint ventures, and so forth.

There is an important lesson here for multinational firms that wish to improve their management of foreign operations through managers who possess a 'global' mentality – i.e. those who can function effectively abroad because they have the technical competence, cultural sensitivity, adaptability and language skills, and are prepared to learn from the locals rather than merely telling them what to do. Multinational firms might begin to tap into these qualities by employing a more culturally diverse workforce at home. Management positions in many western multinationals are held predominantly by white Christian males – in societies which, unlike Japan (an eastern source of many multinational firms), are remarkably multicultural. 'Diversity management' in North America is beginning to address this problem (see for example Jackson, 1992; Ferris *et al.*, 1993). A multicultural workforce would enrich their stock of multicultural skills and knowledge and create an earlier start to global awareness for international assignments than the current practice of offering hurriedly organized cultural awareness programmes and 'learn-a-language-in-two-weeks' courses. Below we consider a relatively neglected aspect of the IHRM context: developing or emergent economies.

The developing country and 'emerging economy' context

The international HRM literature has witnessed a disproportionate emphasis on the US, Japan and now, increasingly, Europe (mostly UK, Germany and France). In their review of 338 articles, Clark *et al.* (1999) found that these five countries accounted for 48 per cent of all cases. This practice echoes Ohmae's (1989) so-called 'Triad' of North America, Europe and Asia–Pacific. Ohmae talked enthusiastically of a 'borderless world' in which country of origin and location of the headquarters does not matter. He hypothesized that

omits. Africa /S. American

information instead would play a pivotal role in realizing this brave new world. The prevalence of the Internet suggests that these predictions were not too far-fetched. However, as Mabey *et al.* (1998: 99) have argued, multinational corporations (MNCs) 'remain embedded in particular national and cultural milieux and carry with them features of their parent-country environment'. This attests to the strength of national orientation and the effect of local ownership interests on the behaviour of multinationals. This is in turn reflected in the trend in theorizing in HRM which has remained ethnocentric, focusing on prescriptive rather than analytical models (e.g. Brewster *et al.*, 1996).

Much research on international HRM has inadvertently or otherwise served the interests of the 'Triad' in the way it seeks to help them understand 'foreign' and in some cases hostile environments, particularly in third world economies. This kind of research pays very little attention to the specific local contextual circumstances that directly impinge on the people who work and live there. This narrow perspective is exacerbated by the practice of replicating research previously conducted in the developed economies. Typically, researchers will merely circulate questionnaires and apply research tools that have been developed and tested elsewhere.

It is doubtful whether this practice advances knowledge in international HRM if we are not given an incisive analysis of the relevant contextual circumstances, in particular the socio-cultural, politico-economic and competitive factors and how they impact on management practice (see also Poole, 1990, 1999). There is now a growing corpus of knowledge that considers the specific problems of the developing country context and which addresses the impact of contextual factors on the management of people within those regions. Some major works include Kiggundu (1989), Jaeger and Kanungo (1990), Budhwar and Debrah (in press) and, more specifically with regard to Africa, Blunt and Jones (1992) and Kamoche (2000a).

In their definition of 'developing countries', Napier and Vu (1998) include countries whose economic development is still in the 'early growth stages' and which typically achieve growth rates averaging 7 per cent and above. This includes many Asian and some Latin American countries. They also talk about 'transitional economies', i.e. those moving from centrally planned to market-oriented economies, such as the former Soviet Union and Eastern Europe, China, etc.

Asian economies have attracted a lot of attention with the emergence of the so-called 'tiger economies' in the 1980s, which saw countries like Thailand, Malaysia and South Korea achieve unprecedented economic growth rates, thus giving a new meaning to the term 'emerging economies'. The economic transformation in East and South East Asia suffered a setback in 1997 after it became clear that the rapid growth had been built on shaky economic foundations, exacerbated by weak financial controls, property speculation and endemic corruption. Thus, while the boom years brought about prosperity, optimism and high incomes, the subsequent fallout has seen widespread organizational restructuring, high unemployment, social strife and political turbulence.

Human resource management researchers who are interested in this region have recognized the need to pay careful attention to contextual factors, including the social–cultural and institutional factors. For example, Confucian influences are widely recognized as playing an important role in shaping organizational behaviour, interpersonal relations, business negotiations, and economic activity in general (e.g. Hofstede and Bond, 1988; Redding, 1990; Tung, 1996). Two of the most important attributes are *guanxi* (connections/networks) (e.g. Tsui and Fahr, 1997) and the concept of face (e.g. Kim and Nam, 1998). These deeply entrenched cultural attributes provide fertile ground in which to formulate human resource strategies and practices that are consistent with the unique circumstances in this region, and which also serve to critique the universalism inherent in much of the mainstream literature. Researchers have identified the crucial role of contextual factors like location, organizational size, ownership, socio-economic factors etc. in a number of Asian countries, from China (e.g. Warner, 1995; Ding *et al.*, 2000) to the advanced economies of South Korea (e.g. Dastmalchian *et al.*, 2000) and Hong Kong (e.g. Fields *et al.*, 2000).

Many observers seem at a loss as to where to locate Africa, since, in the terms of Napier and Vu's classification, many African countries have neither been growing at rapid rates nor are they emerging from the stagnation of centralized planning. With the exception of a few countries like Uganda, Egypt and Cote d'Ivoire which achieved growth rates of 5–6 per cent in the late 1990s, the majority of African economies have seen growth stagnate (or decline) at less than 2 per cent. This has enormous implications for African people, many of whom have seen their incomes diminish in real terms. In a large proportion of sub-Saharan countries for example, up to 50 per cent of the population is considered to be living below the poverty line.

This includes rural people who survive on basic subsistence agriculture, or farmers who have seen the producer prices of their cash crops decline on the world markets, and urban populations who believe they are escaping from poverty to a better life in the cities but end up living in slums with little hope of formal employment. The situation has not been helped by the frequent warfare which has devastated communities from Burundi and Rwanda to the Congo, Somalia, Algeria and Angola. Ordinary people thus find themselves torn between warring factions and adverse weather conditions which can cause untold misery through drought, floods and famine. A small percentage of the population enjoys middle-class lifestyles facilitated by good education, business opportunities and employment.

The human resource challenge therefore assumes a totally new complexion from that normally painted in the mainstream literature. Issues like the needs of multinational firms, or the well-being of expatriates, while obviously important, pale in significance from the point of view of the domestic personnel who consider themselves lucky just to have a job in the first place. Human resource researchers have not shown much interest in these matters, preferring to leave them to aid-donors and social workers. However, there is now a growing awareness that it is impossible, and indeed strategically naïve, for multinational firms to continue to ignore the social and economic context of those affected by their business activities.

The activities of Shell in Nigeria are a case in point – global pressure and a socio-political backlash are ultimately factored into the international business equation. It is not enough to create jobs and pay better wages than local firms. The social agenda will inevitably encroach on the human resource agenda. This requires multinational firms to take a more proactive and inclusive approach in their appropriative ventures in developing countries. This is not unfamiliar territory to the multinationals, as the power of lobby groups in the developed countries – from environmental to consumer protection – amply demonstrates.

Appropriation in an international context

It is suggested here that there is unrealized scope to take the IHRM debate to a new level of sophistication – the generation and leveraging of knowledge across borders outside the straitjacket of common assumptions about the inevitable value of 'globalization'. A critique of globalization is presented below. Here we consider some possible future directions for IHRM. It is necessary first of all to consider the rationale for leveraging learning or disseminating knowledge across subsidiaries or affiliated units. In their analysis, Bartlett and Ghoshal (1989) argue that the benefits of this form of leveraging can be realized through transfers of managers, teamwork, networking, and by sharing information on innovative activities. In this regard they cite firms like Procter and Gamble, Ericsson and NEC. The institution of integrative mechanisms that involve harnessing KSAs ultimately ensures that added value is appropriated by the organization.

The problems of appropriating added value noted in a previous chapter inevitably intensify in the broader, global context where direct control over subsidiaries cannot be guaranteed. Managers are inevitably asking themselves: how can we overcome the constraints – cultural, economic, and even political – that exist in the international competitive arena in order to reap maximum benefits from our investments and operations abroad? An enormous amount of attention has been devoted to this question in the international management and strategic management debates. Within HRM, the issue appears to have been touched on obliquely through 'the effective management of expatriates'. This is surprising given the fact that the financial thrust of foreign direct investments is in the majority of cases underpinned by a strong motivation to secure returns as rapidly and as efficiently as possible.

This is in part due to the perceived uncertainties in international business and unpredictable competitive pressures. Multinational firms operating in new and emergent markets such as Africa, Eastern Europe, South America and parts of Asia often face volatile political and social environments that cannot only make day-to-day business very frustrating but also place the very existence of the operation at risk. Riots, revolutions, political clampdowns, military coups and similar upheavals are some of the events that have taken place in emergent and transitional economies such as Pakistan, Indonesia, Russia and Ecuador in the recent past. In these circumstances, organizations invariably resort to tried and tested financial controls to achieve and retain control over foreign operations.

Multinational firms possess or have access to an impressive arsenal of tools and strategies for strengthening their appropriative capacities. These include intellectual property rights protection; accounting procedures like transfer pricing; creating symbiotic relationships with powerful local politicians, and shifting operations to capitalize on lowest available production and labour costs. The effectiveness of each of these mechanisms is, however, highly variable: in some countries property rights infringements are commonplace; similarly, the changing fortunes of political and military elites are a constant source of uncertainty. Seeking out low labour cost territories is the one notable appropriative mechanism that is easily acknowledged as directly pertinent to HRM. This is a measure that is clearly in the interest of the multinational which is able to neutralize concerns about its 'responsibility' to keep jobs as it seeks to exploit low-cost advantages.

This is exemplified by US and Canadian firms that have abandoned their traditional high wage-cost markets for the more competitive, albeit sufficiently skilled, countries like Mexico, and Japanese firms that have shifted major operations to countries like Thailand, while Hong Kong manufacturing has virtually relocated to mainland China. While these relocations lead to domestic concerns about job loss, the firms in question are able to justify their actions purely on the basis of business considerations – remaining as viable corporate entities answerable to shareholders takes precedence over any implied responsibility to create and keep jobs. If they are unable or unwilling to grasp the opportunities available in low-cost economies, retribution from global competition is normally swift and decisive. Technological advancements have opened new forms of operation which for a technology firm might involve locating software design in India and assembly in Malaysia, coordinating marketing from Singapore, and so forth, thus capitalizing on resources where they are most readily and efficiently available. The issue of 'exporting jobs' thus becomes even more complex.

The entry of concepts like learning and knowledge into the international management debate paves the way for a more explicit treatment of issues attendant on appropriation. In the case of managers on international assignments, appropriation in the international context raises an additional problem: how does the individual manager deal with multiple allegiances/commitments? Commitment to the parent company *vis-à-vis* the subsidiary or affiliate is expected of the parent-country national. Assuring and protecting corporate interests is a central rationale for using expatriates in the first place. Black *et al.* (1992) suggest that firms might try to turn their expatriate managers into 'dual citizens'. Differences are likely to arise when host-country managers espouse ideas which are at odds with those of the expatriates. Hence, the appropriation regime goes beyond the individual–corporate interest level and the apportionment of benefits. The scenario is complicated further where the parent company takes a highly differential approach in its treatment of local and foreign personnel. Not only does this potentially engender resentment in the case of the former; it also raises the risk of their developing a more instrumental and self-interested approach in their dealings with the organization if they believe they are being denied benefits and opportunities. This is often a source of tension in multinational firms (e.g. Leung *et al.*, 1996).

The appropriation–learning perspective (Kamoche and Mueller, 1998) offers some insights into how the shortcomings of a unidimensional approach to appropriation can be resolved. In the area of training, for example, the multinational firm might adopt a more explicit view about the outcomes of the knowledge-base generated in the course of its international activities. Scholars have long debated the application of Perlmutter's typology (ethnocentric–polycentric–regiocentric–geocentric) to issues like staffing policies. This typology suggests, for example, that the geocentric firm develops and deploys its managers purely based on merit and individual potential, with no consideration given to extraneous factors like national/geographic origin. If this approach is indeed tenable, this might go some way towards re-assuring host-country nationals that their interests in the appropriative regime are being taken care of, including opportunities for career advancement.

In reality, however, the geocentric model remains an untenable ideal except for a very small number of firms and only among a small cadre of high-flying managers. Furthermore, while the potential benefits of leveraging learning may appear obvious to the objective observer, from the point of view of the multinational firm the reality may be quite different. In the previous chapter we considered some of the difficulties of appropriating tacit knowledge. We continue the debate here by noting that many organizations are increasingly striving to codify certain aspects of knowledge through management structures or operating systems, or simply through the increased use of technology. Thus, if organizations develop the capability to codify tacit knowledge, this diminishes the individual's appropriative capacities.

This implies that expatriates can be seen not merely as the critical linchpins in the organization's knowledge-leveraging structure, but as facilitators and implementers of some specific business strategy. Thus, they will be valued more for their ability to institute mechanisms to ensure organizational self-reproduction. They are deployed to do a job, and when the job is done, they are simply relocated not just where their expertise is most needed, but where the organization is still facing obstacles to its self-reproduction and appropriative regime. The organization weighs the cost of expatriating a parent-country national who can also ensure corporate control against that of hiring a host-country national whose first allegiance is likely to be the subsidiary firm. This shows the extent to which human resource considerations can easily be subordinated to business and corporate control objectives. Expatriates who have found themselves marginalized on return, unable to find an appropriate posting in a reorganized home operation, may well identify with this sharp edge of the corporate appropriation knife.

Globalization: reality or false promise?

It seems appropriate to conclude this international HRM discussion with a more general look at the globalization debate and
how it has impacted on HRM. The inexorable move toward world
economic integration has been debated throughout the twentieth
century since Norman Angell wrote his bestseller *The Great
Illusion* in 1910. Angell argued that international finance, trade
and industry were becoming so interdependent that power would
eventually shift away from governments to industry.

This is precisely the logic that has today underpinned the
globalization debate. From the mid-1990s, globalization has come
to be lauded as the great new wave to lead us all into a bright new
future of advanced technology, free trade and a convergence that
would make all national systems and organizations resemble each
other. The integration of financial markets which today facilitates
the instantaneous movement of funds on the information super-
highway comes closest to illustrating the irrelevance of national
borders.

This was amply demonstrated in the wake of the Asian economic crisis in 1997, particularly with regard to currency speculation by 'hedge funds'. A high degree of fluidity is also being
achieved in the movement of goods, especially with the onset of e-
commerce. The physical movement of people still encounters fric-
tion on account of restrictions on immigration, reluctance to
relocate, adaptation problems and other related personal costs of
mobility, high costs of repatriation, domestic pressures for localization, and suchlike. Furthermore, the 'internationalization' of
managers has not materialized to the extent previously anticipated, certainly with regard to the UK (Forster, 2000).

National business structures are built upon socio-cultural,
politico-economic and technological foundations that must be
understood in a historical context. These will not change easily in
the wake of global trends. The corporate interrelationships and
long-term perspective in the Japanese business system have
largely remained in place in spite of global pressures for reform
and for the form of shareholder participation usually associated
with western capitalism. Britain still refuses to be swept into a supposedly homogenizing Europe. Across the world, globalization

has been resisted by calls for the rejection of 'foreign values'; the need to protect national sovereignty and other such manifestations of nationalism; the raising of trade barriers; localization of the workforce, and so forth.

Where wide-ranging reforms have been instigated by globalization including pressure from institutions like the World Bank and the International Monetary Fund (IMF), the results have fallen far short of expectations. This has been the case in African countries that were subjected to structural adjustment programmes which, while facilitating the continuance of foreign aid, have also been blamed for the escalation of poverty, high unemployment and social strife. Earlier doubts about the value of globalization have gradually culminated in the realization that the internationalization of business practices, the convergence of markets and the rapid restructuring of economic systems can all have a very deleterious effect on the most vulnerable members of society particularly in poor countries. The all too familiar demonstrations and riots at recent international meetings of the World Trade Organization in Seattle, the World Economic Forum in Davos, United Nations Conference on Trade and Development (UNCTAD) in Bangkok and the IMF/World Bank in London demonstrate the general public's growing dissatisfaction with globalization.

These belligerent public reactions to globalization represent a more explicit demand for social consciousness on the part of international capitalism. They constitute a rejection of contemporary appropriative mechanisms available to multinational firms and other international organizations such as the Bretton Woods institutions (World Bank and IMF). Although it is tempting to see these events merely within the context of economics, it is suggested here that they impinge heavily on a social agenda which includes the effects of organizations and global institutions on the day-to-day lives of ordinary people. The international human resource agenda is inevitably tied into this debate through the use of expatriates to effect business strategies and/or economic policies and through the direct impact of such strategies/policies on the host-country workforce.

This applies equally to the more obvious case of international trade. Where firms in poor countries are denied access to lucrative western markets, and yet at the same time find themselves pitted against powerful multinationals on their own turf, the issues begin to go beyond the familiar cries of 'protectionism' and begin to take on an ominous complexion. It quickly becomes clear that trade is not all that free, and the proponents of globalization are coming under pressure to demonstrate that they are not merely being driven by self-interest. This is a tall order for business, since shareholder interests inevitably take precedence.

The question is: is it possible for firms in the global arena to sustain a viable balance between their self-interests and those of other relevant stakeholders? Put differently, how can individual countries embrace the integrative forces of globalization while retaining their nation-specific identities and sources of competitive advantage? This will be one of the most difficult challenges in the twenty-first century. The IHRM research agenda will inevitably have to go beyond the current parochial concerns with the interests of MNCs and expatriation/repatriation and begin to evaluate the effects of global activities on host-country workforces, and other critical issues such as the role of the local contextual factors (including locally available expertise) on the formulation of business and human resource strategies.

We have argued that the question of managing people needs to extend its current reach. In the next chapter we consider whether business, be it domestic or global, can begin to address these questions more fully by adopting a broader social agenda.

MANAGING IN A SOCIAL CONTEXT

In our efforts to understand *human resource management*, it is helpful to pause a little and consider the implications of the *managing*
aspect of this expression. After all, our discussion has so far con-
centrated on the *human resource*, which is one part of the equation.
The purpose here is not to embark on a discourse in semantics but
only to raise a number of questions which might help us better
understand the full implications of HRM. This chapter considers
the suitability of the concept of a community and ponders
whether in such communities the idea of *facilitation* might be an
appropriate way to conceive of the task of 'managing people'. The
idea of 'facilitating' is not new; it is hoped, however, that its treatment within a robust social context might generate some new
insights into this complex phenomenon of HRM.

The increasing complexity of the global competitive arena
clearly calls for a full rethink about the role of organizations in the
management of people. In fact, from a critical perspective, the idea
of 'managing people' itself needs re-examining. When we begin to
ponder what it really means to manage people, a number of questions quickly come to the surface, raising some doubt about the
appropriateness of this expression, at least in respect of some cat-
egories of work. Do people need managing? Can they be managed? Who exactly is doing the managing and for what purpose?

I believe these questions lie at the heart of the quest to *understand* what is human resource management and, equally importantly, what it is not. One could go even further to introduce the question of why organizations exist in the first place – a question that has preoccupied scholars in industrial economics and strategic management with regard to the 'firm'. The firm is but one organizational form, and the rationale for its existence clearly differs in some fundamental respects from those of non-profit-making organizations. However, all organizations, be they business corporations, public universities, jazz clubs or charities, are involved in this task of organizing productive activities through human skills and knowledge. It follows therefore that they have an inescapable responsibility to comprehend the full implications of this exercise.

Increasingly, the organization is being seen as a social community, rather than merely an institution for maximizing shareholder wealth. According to Kogut and Zander (1996: 503) the firm can be understood 'as a social community specializing in the speed and efficiency in the creation and transfer of knowledge'. While this cannot be interpreted as a diminution of shareholder interests, the notion of a community invokes certain social tenets that are routinely ignored in the purely economic conception of organizations.

As I noted in Chapter 6, the creation of knowledge is rapidly being recognized as one of the most important activities that organizations engage in – it is in fact the beginning of a new paradigm for theorizing the nature of organizations, according to some authors (e.g. Grant, 1996; Spender, 1996). The emergent knowledge school of thought acknowledges that the creation of knowledge is geared to some specific ends, of which the realization of added value is one of the most readily recognized. This raises two points which I consider important from a human resource management point of view: one, much of this knowledge-creation process constitutes of intellectual capital (which in turn is grounded in the notion of human capital); two, the creation of knowledge takes place in social settings which involve such human factors as social interaction and networking, relationships, trust, sharing and so forth. Of course there are a myriad other relevant contexts, e.g. the technological, competitive forces, the politico-economic, etc. This chapter considers the relevance of the social context with particular regard to the extent to which the organization's social agenda can be expanded to take account of emergent exigencies that impact directly on people.

Organizations as communities

It is now recognized that the organizational context provides an environment in which members seek to establish mutually beneficial relationships as social actors rather than merely to work. The dynamics of the social context have been recognized from the earliest contributions to organizational socialization (e.g. Van Maanen and Schein, 1979). More recently, researchers have examined the factors that bring people together, for example within the context of social networks theory (e.g. Ibarra, 1992; Brass, 1995). Focusing on the relationships rather than the personal attributes of social actors, Brass (1995: 72) argues that the role of human resource managers is that of 'brokers bringing together a mix of people to successfully offer a product or service'. Mueller (1996: 777) proposes a shift away from 'culture' to 'social architecture' which arises from 'ongoing skill formation activities, incidental or informal learning, forms of spontaneous cooperation' and tacit knowledge. This section builds on these insights to explore the suitability of the view that an organizational context might be viewed as a community and what implications this raises for HRM.

About thirty years ago, in an analysis of management problems in Africa, Onyemelukwe (1973) proposed an expanded role for organizations within what he termed 'the community concept of business'. He saw this as the answer to the failure of business methods to address fully the psychological needs of those most affected by them. According to this perspective, the individual would be treated as part of a community to which he/she agreed to be a member by choice. Such a community would be built on 'close interpersonal relationships and group interactions welded by a feeling of security and harmony, on the part of all its members. The members submit themselves and their hopes to this community' (1973: 123).

113

Some features of such a community include:

- a governance structure based on fairness and transparency;
- reciprocal values of respect within the authority structure;
- recognition of certain aspects of personal status valued by the community, in addition to the concern for productivity;
- a consideration of the community's holistic values in human resource decisions;
- legitimizing a system of welfare paternalism to engender loyalty.

These propositions were put forward at a time when managers were seen as remote, unapproachable and autocratic. Much progress has been made over the years in improving managerial attitudes and practices, and this seems to be an appropriate time to revisit the concept of a community in order to determine what contribution it can make to redefining a social context of business.

Within such a community, management practices become compatible with the extant cultural practices, working with them rather than against them to foster 'harmonious settings' which Onyemelukwe believed prevailed in Africa. Whether 'African settings' are harmonious is debatable; the important question is: are such communities viable and do people want to be members of such communities, not just in Africa but elsewhere? This question is particularly pertinent to the organizational climate in many organizations around the world today in which a highly individualistic ethos sits uneasily beside a collectivist one. On the one hand, people are encouraged to demonstrate their individual capabilities and are rewarded on merit; on the other hand, they are exhorted to see themselves as members of high-performing teams.

The idea of a community of which one actively wants to be a member is appealing because presumably it does not involve coercion, and it also leaves open the opportunity for voluntary exit. Also, by emphasizing community values, it offers a way toward resolving the above paradox since such values could include both individual and team elements by mutual agreement. Transparency thus plays a vital role: eliminating the ambiguities and grey areas that often shroud company policies and lead to accusations of unfairness and favouritism. The issue of loyalty is a little more problematic. An extreme interpretation of the appropriation debate might lead one to the conclusion that commitment or loyalty to the organization are rendered meaningless by the narrow pursuit of self-interest.

However, as we argued previously, the availability of a learning trajectory and opportunities for career advancement, as well as fairness and clarity in the mechanisms for the distribution of benefits, can form the basis for a viable relationship between the individual and the organization. If we then extend the debate into a broader social context, it is conceivable therefore that, to the extent that people want to be part of a community as defined above, they will share in its aspirations for success because these aspirations are consistent with their own and they are proactively involved in generating and sustaining them. This may well include developing a sense of loyalty to that community. Non-profit organizations and some high-tech environments seem to be able to sustain community tenets well.

Research areas such as organizational commitment and culture have endeavoured to identify the sorts of circumstances that might engender such congenial settings. A whole range of other topics have added their voice to the debate, including the quality of working life movement, empowerment, gainsharing and so forth. Many of these initiatives are supposed to be engineered by managers, and do not clearly specify a proactive role for the joint stakeholder – the people. One important assumption underpinning these developments is that showing some consideration for people is not inimical to the achievement of organizational objectives. Social reformers and other proponents of humanizing work have always recognized that this sort of consideration makes good business sense. In recent years, this thinking has no doubt benefited from developments in related areas of social responsibility, such as environmental protection, 'customer-is-king' claims in marketing, and consumer protection.

These developments reflect an effort on the part of the corporate world to achieve a better rapprochement with the social world. As such, the pursuit of business objectives need not be at the expense of social goals. Such goals include a commitment to progressive human resource initiatives which not only involve developing people through training, but also take a proactive approach to improve the social conditions that affect their working lives. While this effort can be said to have yielded some notable outcomes in some quarters, for many, especially in emergent and developing economies, much still remains to be done. In fact, questions are now being asked about the ethics of HRM (e.g. Rosen and Juris, 1995) and also whether there are moral obligations on organizations to give people a positive experience of working or whether all activities must be judged on utilitarianism (e.g. Miller, 1996; Legge, 1997).

From a philosophical viewpoint, utilitarianism judges the moral worth of actions in terms of the utility of their consequences for all relevant stakeholders (Snell, 1999). The question that arises is whether the organization's obligations to its stakeholders should stop at a simple 'win–win' perspective. This would create the problem whereby employees are judged merely in terms of their 'objectively' observable actions and how these contribute to the bottom line. At its most extreme, it entails cutting out all those who are not seen as contributing to financial performance, as opposed to taking an approach more consistent with nurturing in order to bring out whatever hidden talents they might have.

Many organizations around the world are still guilty of neglecting the social outcomes of their business actions either by polluting the environment, or failing to show due concern about the negative effects of their products on people. The tobacco industry is a case in point. Thus there appears to be a paradox: while they may be instituting progressive human resource practices (including good salaries and medical schemes) for their own employees, many organizations are ignoring the broader social constituency within which these same employees actually exist. It is as if people can be thought to have dislodged themselves from their everyday lives when they arrive at the factory or office. The connection between work and social life is not left in abeyance every time we go to work. In any case, emergent practices like flexitime and telecommuting, as well as new developments in organizational structure and design such as organizations without boundaries and virtual organizations, would all seem to suggest a further blurring of traditional demarcations in the way we think about organizations. Viewed from this perspective, the charge for a broadening of the corporate social agenda does not, hopefully, seem that far-fetched.

The idea of constructing a community calls to mind previous efforts to humanize work, so in that sense it is not being offered here as a revolutionary concept. As far as Onyemelukwe's variant is concerned, what is notable about it is that it was being offered in response to perceived failures of business, hence as a mechanism for rectifying and modifying some deeply entrenched practices. Thus, it aspired to the realms of sustainable and lasting social reform as opposed to merely seeking to achieve some incremental changes in organizational practice at the micro level. Without taking a broad-brush universalist position, it is fair to say that Onyemelukwe's propositions could probably have some relevance in other parts of the world to various degrees.

The identification of the problem of appropriation is consistent with the critique of unitarism and the recognition that existing frameworks for theorizing human resource management such as the quest for 'fit' do not sufficiently address the socio-psychological let alone the political dimensions of 'managing' people. The onset of globalization has brought the shortcomings of business into sharper focus, and it is our contention here that this will increasingly become a major bone of contention in the twenty-first century as organizations play a more visible and irrevocable role in the lives of a multiplicity of stakeholders (see also Schuler, forthcoming). And yet the necessity for organizations is not in question. What is at issue is whether organizations are sufficiently equipped to handle the challenges of the social context that they are in part responsible for bringing about.

It is not anticipated here that human resource managers will be required to turn into social reformers or even social workers. In fact whatever it is that goes into the task of managing people need not be seen as the exclusive domain of human resource managers. This point has been recognized by those who call for more involvement of line managers by arguing that line managers are best placed to understand what actually goes on at the workplace. What this ultimately does is to redefine the social responsibility of *all* managers on a much wider scale than has been the case so far. Line managers have always had some human resource responsibilities, such as interviewing job candidates, carrying out performance appraisal, identifying training needs and firing people. It might therefore have appeared somewhat strange to many of them when researchers began calling for line management involvement in HRM. 'We've been doing this all along!' might have been an apt response. In reality, what these writers were proposing was that the human resource responsibilities should be acknowledged as central features of the task of managing, rather than something line managers did on an ad hoc and piecemeal basis (see also Storey, 1992).

This implies that the human resource or personnel department/function need not be seen as the social conscience of the organization. It is the overall managerial task that requires a reappraisal, in order that managers, in whatever capacity, might be able to appreciate the full implications of what it means to manage people in a context in which traditional institutional arrangements are coming under closer scrutiny. Tyson (1995) also anticipates more involvement of *all* managers in dealing with the social challenges faced by organizations.

If all those in a managerial capacity perceived a social contract between themselves individually and the relevant stakeholders, the community concept would begin to take shape. A social contract would build on existing notions of the psychological contract while recognizing that the relationship between the individual and the organization should not only be apprehended at the psychological but at the sociological level as well. A social contract would more suitably lend itself to an analysis of the philosophical, political and ethical components of the employment relationship and is potentially more inclusive of the multiplicity of stakeholders.

Facilitating knowledge creation and resourcefulness

If individuals opt to become members of organizations, it is fair to say that they also take on a responsibility to maintain a viable relationship between themselves and that organization. At the most basic level, they agree to abide by the organization's governance regime as spelt out in the rules and regulations. However, this by itself does not make a community. Resorting to work-to-rules by aggrieved individuals can make a mockery of the governance structure. Similarly, as the industrial relations literature demonstrates, ambiguity as to the substance and scope of the governance structure itself has historically been a major source of contention and conflict. The notion of mutual obligations needs to be taken into account when exploring the wider implications of the appropriation regime. This takes the employment relationship one step further – away from the unidimensional view of organizations managing people to a much more radical and potentially controversial scenario in which both the individual and the organization are jointly responsible for *managing* (for want of a better word) the stock of knowledge they are jointly generating.

Such a scenario goes beyond popular conceptions of empowerment in which the organization hands out quantities of autonomy. More than ever before, the business world evolves around information and the capacity to generate and utilize new knowledge. As we argued in Chapter 6, the knowledge that is generated by and through people contains a large tacit component. Polanyi (1962), who is widely credited with clarifying the distinction between tacit and explicit knowledge, believed that some aspects of knowledge would inevitably remain tacit. We can call this the *residual tacit component of knowledge*. This residual component remains in spite of existing mechanisms to codify knowledge and make it explicit.

While arguing that some aspects of knowledge are non-codifiable, we must leave open the possibility that the mechanisms for achieving greater degrees of codifying knowledge have not yet been discovered or invented. As we noted in an earlier chapter, the limited scope to codify tacit knowledge has far-reaching implications for HRM, in terms of appropriation. It is suggested here that the argument can be developed further within the social context, and in particular with regard to the creation of social capital. In a recent paper, Nahapiet and Ghoshal (1998: 243) have argued that social capital is 'the sum of the actual and potential resources embedded within, available through and derived from the network of relationships possessed by an individual or social unit'.

Networks of personal relationships are an important building block of social capital, which points to the importance of the 'community'. Indeed, some writers have identified the importance of elements like trust, cooperation, respect, mutual obligations, friendship and so forth in the creation of social capital and prosperity (e.g. Bourdieu, 1986; Fukuyama, 1995). These elements of social capital are in essence tacit, and efforts to codify them would be either very difficult or ludicrous. While it may be possible for an investment agent to list down names and contact details of prospective clients that are currently being 'courted', if such an agent left the firm it would be difficult for another agent merely to carry on with these same prospects, especially if the 'courting' was based on mutual, interpersonal trust and was conducted informally, outside the formal environment of the office.

This in part explains why such advisers/consultants are prone to migrate with their client base. The same can be said for other professions that involve networks of clients, collaborators and so on, such as auditors/accountants, bankers, lawyers, academic researchers etc. Following Nelson and Winter's (1982) distinction between skills and routines, we suggest that while routines can be used to represent the codifiable aspects of knowledge, the requisite skills for task accomplishment can be difficult to pass on or even communicate. Thus, one may study a blueprint, recipe or formula prepared (codified) by someone else and be unable to effect it, let alone understand it. It shows there is a tacit component to the nature of work which is appropriable by the individual. It also shows the complexity inherent in the organization as a community and in particular the difficulties managers are likely to encounter in trying to manage the social relations attendant on the creation of knowledge.

This takes the discussion in a new direction: should managers be trying to *manage* a phenomenon that appears manifestly unmanageable? Perhaps we should not be talking of *managing per se*. The word itself connotes some inherent values and is ideologically loaded. Furthermore, given its unitarist application, its appropriateness in a pluralist community context is suspect. It is not being proposed here that a mere change of name is all that is needed; indeed, name changes can be woefully inadequate, often resulting in cosmetic treatment of otherwise profound issues. What is needed is a change of mentality and a basic acknowledgement that the existing frameworks for managing people are ripe for a radical shake-up in the knowledge era.

A good starting point is the notion of *facilitation*. This has been proposed before in leadership theory. For example, in participative leadership styles, the role of the leader is facilitation and communication (e.g. Hersey and Blanchard, 1988). Facilitation has also been recognized as a possible strategy for overcoming resistance to change (e.g. Kotter and Schlesinger, 1979). We build on these arguments to offer the notion of *facilitating* the resourcefulness and creativity that exist in individuals or networks (including teams) of people who constitute knowledge communities. Such a shift in thinking would also help unleash the 'resourcefulness' that resides in people, and which underpins the view that people constitute a 'resource'.

Facilitation implies that managers acknowledge that human action at the organizational level manifests itself in individual choice, innovativeness and a capacity to create (Kamoche, 1996b). The task for managers therefore is to enable the realization of this capacity to create – this is the resourcefulness inherent in human *resources*. In a similar vein, Spender (1996: 47) argues that top management should 'provide a context in which employees at every level become independent agents, take responsibility, experiment and make mistakes and learn as they strive for continuous improvement in every aspect of the firm's total transformation process'.

The current Internet explosion and associated organizational initiatives to foster creativity are in essence efforts to tap into 'resourcefulness'. As Penrose (1959) noted, the underutilized resources in the organization constitute future opportunities for growth. According to her, the value of a resource lies in its potential to yield a service. If people are hired for their perceived or proven ability to generate a 'service' for the organization, then their knowledge, skills and abilities must be seen as a potential source of individual and organizational 'growth'.

The parallel in the technology literature is how firms develop new applications from existing knowledge. According to Schumpeter ([1911] 1968), innovations come about through combinations of existing knowledge and by achieving production through different methods. Thus, firms 'learn' by finding new ways to do things and by the incremental application of new knowledge to existing capabilities. Kogut and Zander (1992) refer to this as the firm's 'combinative capabilities' which allow firms to generate new applications from existing knowledge.

In their conception of knowledge, Nonaka and Takeuchi (1995: 226) have argued that it is the social interaction between tacit and explicit knowledge that leads to the creation of knowledge. They point out that in the Japanese context where tacit knowledge takes precedence, 'the tendency is to overemphasize the use of figurative language and symbolism at the expense of a more analytical approach and documentation', such as that favoured in western epistemology.

The challenge lies in reaching into the complex social context in which the scope for 'resourcefulness' is embedded and which, as noted above, is largely tacit and non-codifiable. Sporting activities provide useful illustration: in team sports like football and basketball, it is not just the skills of individual players that matter, but their ability to gell. Their knowledge of each other's strengths and weaknesses is just as important as their own self-knowledge. The mechanisms they have invented for communicating in action, the existence of sufficient levels of trust, their ability to render support and share in the joys and tribulations of winning and losing are examples of the socially embedded threads of the fabric that holds such groups together, ensuring a high degree of motivation for consistent performance. In the performing arts like jazz improvization, similar social structures exist alongside the technical issues such as performative competence and an understanding of one's instrument (e.g. Bastien and Hostager, 1988; Weick, 1998; Cunha *et al.*, 1999; Hatch, 1999).

Sharing and communicating knowledge may be facilitated by learning a set of values that allows individuals to communicate through a shared language (Berger and Luckmann, 1967). It may also depend on the extent to which such individuals are willing and prepared to share knowledge, whether adequate incentives exist for doing so, and what interests are at stake. For example, is the sharing of knowledge rewarded or do people feel they have too much to lose by sharing, which would in turn lead them to take a proprietorial view over their skills and competencies and begin acting self-interestedly? Are people unduly penalized for mistakes which then discourages them from further experimentation and information sharing?

It cannot be taken for granted that people will always be willing to share knowledge or that they will always want to belong to communities in which knowledge sharing is a fundamental norm. Not only are they faced with opportunities to act in their own interest, they are also likely to act in competition with the organization in generating and utilizing knowledge. Realizing a robust community is therefore rendered somewhat more challenging by the fact that organizations are engaged in a politically charged task of generating knowledge – using technology, skills and other resources to solve problems and generate new products and services. This does not in itself make such a task impossible; instead, it serves to highlight the fact that understanding the nature of human resources will not follow any hard and fast rules. It is an ongoing process that requires us to be constantly aware of the various ways in which the phenomenon manifests itself.

The need for a new perspective

An overriding theme in HRM is that the organization can count on the individual's willing collaboration in developing and providing products and services. When this fails, such an individual can expect to face sanctions, including the risk of losing his or her job. Agency theory and developments in empowerment have gone some way toward generating solutions. The problem of 'managing' tacit knowledge makes the task of the organization even more difficult. This is why new solutions must now be sought in new directions. This will involve exploring alternative theoretical frameworks and re-examining the usefulness of existing ones. By locating the discussion within a social context, this chapter aims to generate some interest in research paradigms which question the relevance and utility of some of the taken-for-granted assumptions underpinning the theory and practice of management.

Such an approach will also involve a fresh look at the question of power – how it is constituted and utilized in the knowledge era (a.k.a. information age), and the ways in which the locus of power is shifting towards those who best understand the dynamics of the knowledge-creation process; the way knowledge disguises power bases and allows the repositories of knowledge to tilt the power balance in their favour.

The pervasiveness of knowledge up and down the organization

and the inability of management to understand it in its various manifestations – which in turn impacts on their ability to control it – ultimately implies that the legitimacy of a top-down managerial approach comes into question. The seemingly simple axiom 'knowledge is power' assumes an ominous dimension for those attempting to use traditional methods to 'manage' something they do not fully understand. It is indeed difficult to comprehend fully the tacit nature of knowledge that is constantly changing.

At the most basic level, skills do not remain static; they improve or deteriorate according to the demands placed upon people to carry out tasks and solve problems. The turbulence that characterizes the business world today forces organizations to evince their adaptability to constant change and prepare their people to do likewise. Where individuals are increasingly judged on their ability to be creative in idea generation, in how they relate to customers, how they design new products and services, and create new methods for solving problems, there needs to be a concomitant approach to the way management facilitates and coordinates these activities.

A context of 'facilitating resourcefulness' takes as its starting point the social circumstances in which people are engaged in the generation and utilization of knowledge, and how these circumstances are in turn affected by political, technological, economic and ethical factors that have all assumed a new meaning in the globally integrated world of business. Thus, human resource management should no longer be seen along the narrow lines of selecting and training people, reward and punishment, etc. Furthermore, its remit must transcend the traditional borders of human resource and personnel departments which still fulfil a 'staff' or advisory function in spite of claims about being equal partners in strategic management.

While such micro-level analyses as selection and training will still be needed, their narrow focus will ring hollow in an increasingly complex world in which organizational reality is defined by an agenda broader than current concerns with productivity. This is also a world in which the role of organizations is increasingly being challenged on ethical, environmental and socio-political grounds as discussed earlier. This is hardly surprising, given the immense power organizations wield today, with many multinational firms commanding market capitalization larger than some countries' GNPs. It may be that organizations will need to redefine their role in society even as they address their strategic objectives and performance imperatives. My purpose has been to show how changing the fundamental rationale for 'managing' people squares with such an eventuality.

9

THE FUTURE OF HRM

Understanding the phenomenon of human resource management in its various manifestations is a difficult task. It is even more challenging to forecast how this phenomenon will continue to change in the future. Global turbulence requires managers to develop a capacity to learn on an ongoing basis, which includes the capacity to challenge their preferred approaches to managing people. Learning within an ever-changing competitive landscape will involve going beyond the practice of benchmarking and being able to determine how best to cope with the surprises that are constantly thrown their way. For example, managers might ponder how best to deal with challenges like the Asian economic crisis whose ramifications are felt far beyond Asia, what new opportunities and problems the internet revolution is likely to spawn, and so forth.

As people become more aware of their rights and more critical of business practices and managerial excesses, they will demand more accountability, more transparency, fairness and a sense of justice. Similarly, as they become more aware of their own abilities and true value to the organization, they will demand more recognition, a greater say in decision making and in how knowledge is generated and utilized. Technology continues to redefine the workplace and indeed the very nature of work itself. It is time we asked ourselves whether the extant management practices are sufficiently equipped to deal with these new developments. The agenda will have to shift away from merely designing good, functional practices to anticipating ways in which the existing and potential resources can be deployed or reconfigured.

Some observers believe there is still a lot of confusion about what HRM is and what it represents. Some hold on to the belief that HRM is essentially an American phenomenon with little applicability elsewhere. No doubt many of the definitive themes in HRM were first given prominence in America; however, if we think of HRM as more than just a set of practices for achieving organizational outcomes, then the geographical origins become less important than the socio-political, cultural, institutional and economic factors that affect managerial behaviour in different parts of the world. Understanding the essence of HRM will necessitate a closer scrutiny of the specific context within which managers develop their chosen approach for managing people.

The common criticism that HRM is just a manifestation of values that are unique to one country partly reflects the manner in which the spirit of HRM has been conveyed. It is erroneous to think of HRM as a uniform set of practices which can be applied like a formula to any human resource problem situation. The implied universal applicability is clearly misplaced. Equally questionable is the belief that all that is needed is a modification of the practices so that they are compatible with the culture in order to ensure the successful implementation of HRM. Considering what is needed and feasible in a particular culture first is a more appropriate approach. Culture is but one consideration, and care must be exercised in talking of transposing practices *from one culture to another*.

The general critique of HRM has taken many shapes and forms, including doubts about its internal coherence, its inherent contradictions, its unitarism, and indeed its hypocrisy. These views have to some extent helped to ensure that the proponents of HRM do not get carried away in their enthusiastic advocacy of a concept that is far from perfect. Some authors have wondered whether these observations are symptomatic of a more serious problem in the conception of the phenomenon. Others suggest there might be a real crisis in HRM. In querying whether a crisis exists in HRM, Sparrow (1998) argues that there has been at least 'a crisis of confidence' in terms of the challenges that have been brought about by the handing over of significant powers to line managers who are ill-equipped to handle the technical and social issues involved in managing people.

This type of environment has in turn engendered a culture in which the proclamations about HR intents are not entirely borne out in reality. In fact, many contradictions result from the failure to align action with intent, or where the language used is deliberately obscure: managers talk of 'rightsizing' when they mean 'downsizing'. According to Sparrow, HR managers have thus become 'disenfranchized' – the potential changes they can make to HR systems are now limited. This should come as no surprise.

Some of the earlier proponents of HRM warned of the paradox that if HR was to be taken seriously, it had to give a substantial part of its responsibilities away to line managers. Whether line managers were suitably prepared or qualified to handle these challenges did not appear to be an issue at the time. It clearly is an issue today. HR practitioners find themselves in an unenviable position in which they are expected by some to be the conscience of the organization, while at the same time implementing painful strategies like downsizing that they have played little or no role in formulating.

Whether or not there is a crisis in HRM, remarkable progress has been made in developing this phenomenon, clarifying its conceptual foundations, designing good practices, enhancing its image, building it into the strategic management process and so forth. Still, much remains to be done. Some observers had predicted the demise of the HR manager as line managers encroached on their territories. HR managers have, in the main, reinvented themselves and ensured their survival.

All managers may well need to reinvent themselves in order to cope better with globalization and the need to take an active role in knowledge creation and utilization. If managers understand their role in terms of facilitating knowledge creation and learning, and fostering an environment in which the various forces involved in knowledge creation (people's skills, organizational capabilities, technology etc.) are allowed to interface constructively, then the entire nature of organizations as we understand them will be seen in a new light.

While doubts remain about the extent to which the interests of the various stakeholders are being suitably mediated, there has at least been an acknowledgement that the tasks and challenges of managing people cannot be relegated to moribund personnel departments. However, the future prospects are not entirely clear. Will human resource decisions continue to be driven by hard-nosed business strategies? Will the value of HR be appreciated in ways other than those that are directly observable and measurable? No doubt researchers will continue to search for new theoretical perspectives for unravelling HRM. New practices will be developed, new methods for problem solving proposed, and new ammunition for challenging the phenomenon created. One thing is certain: there will be no quick fix to resolve the tension between the pressures for performance and the humanization of work.

Directions for further research

The aim of this book was to seek a better understanding of the nature of human resource management and to examine whether the current perspectives and practices are well equipped to handle the increasingly complex nature of this discipline. I have argued that current efforts to understand HRM retain too many elements which are either redundant or represent gaps in the conception of HRM. The preoccupation with 'fit', the neglect of appropriation, and the failure to explore the full implications of the resource-based view are but a few examples. Similarly, researchers have not fully appreciated the implications of the dynamic concept of knowledge within the HRM debate as many still remain wedded to the more mundane issues of competencies, selection, performance appraisal, training and managing expatriates. Of course these are important topics, and we probably still need to discover better ways to design human resource practices. However, the research agenda must now take a broader and more enlightened view.

The role of the human resource practitioners has been changing and will continue to face pressure to change with the times. We need more incisive research into the nature and significance of the globalization of business, including the social–political role organizations play in their areas of operation. Multidisciplinary research might bring together researchers in diverse areas like

HRM, organization theory and political science to achieve a better understanding of the multifaceted nature of the forces of globalization, and how people both shape and are affected by these forces. The diversity of disciplines that today inform the field requires researchers to venture into non-traditional research areas and to be sensitive to the potential interpretations of HRM that these endeavours yield. It is in this regard that concepts like appropriation and knowledge must be viewed. They open new avenues for researching HRM and will clearly be influential in defining the research agenda for HRM in the future.

Whether at the 'domestic' or 'global' level, there will clearly be a need for HRM research to move away from the unidimensional perspective which has resulted from the practice among researchers to restrict their inquiries to managers and those in a supervisory capacity. The voices of other organizational members are not often heard, partly because managers restrict access to subordinates while they hide behind the veil of 'confidentiality'. There is also a belief among researchers that the higher up the organization they go in their quest for answers, the more valid their findings. This is perhaps due to the nature of the information being sought – if researchers are looking for data on things like the formulation of strategies, policies and practices and how these affect HR decisions, the higher echelons are a plausible starting point.

But we shouldn't stop there. Researchers must strike a fine balance between understanding/explaining social phenomena and serving the commercial interests of their informants. When it comes to reconstructing the organizational reality with particular regard to how strategic decisions affect HRM, the perspective of one set of stakeholders is clearly inadequate, if not downright misleading. Researchers will also need to use more appropriate research methodologies. This may involve an eclectic combination of both nomothetic and idiographic methodologies which achieve analytical rigour without sacrificing their explanatory value. Researchers will therefore need to re-examine the suitability of current theories of the firm which draw largely from economics and appear unable to embrace the dynamics of the social context of business, and which are underpinned by a rational–realist epistemology. Human resource management is too important to be addressed unidimensionally.

REFERENCES

Adler, N.J. (1986) *International Dimensions of Organizational Behaviour.* Boston, MA: PWS-Kent.

Adler, N.J. and Ghadar, F . (1990) Strategic human resource management: a global perspective, in R. Pieper (ed.) *Human Resource Management: An International Comparison.* Berlin: Walter de Gruyter.

Alvesson, M. (1993) Organizations as rhetoric: knowledge-intensive firms and the struggle with ambiguity, *Journal of Management Studies,* 30, 997–1016.

Amit, R. and Schoemaker, P.J.H. (1993) Strategic assets and organizational rent, *Strategic Management Journal,* 14, 33–46.

Anderson, L. (2000) Have an MBA – will travel, *Financial Times,* 6 March: 12.

Anthony, P.D. (1977) *The Ideology of Work.* London: Tavistock.

Anthony, P.D. (1994) *Managing Culture.* Buckingham: Open University Press.

Argyris, C. (1993) *Actionable Knowledge.* San Francisco, CA: Jossey-Bass.

Armstrong, M. (1987) Human resource management: a case of the emperor's new clothes, *Personnel Management,* 19(8), 30–5.

Arthur, J.B. (1994) Effects of human resource management systems on manufacturing performance and turnover, *Academy of Management Journal,* 37, 670–87.

Aryee, S. and Stone, R.J. (1996) Work experiences, work adjustment and psychological well-being of expatriate employees in Hong Kong, *International Journal of Human Resource Management,* 7(3), 149–63.

Barley, S. and Kunda, G. (1992) Design and devotion: surges of rational and normative ideologies of control in managerial discourse, *Administrative Science Quarterly*, 37, 363–99.

Barney, J.B. (1986) Organizational culture: can it be a source of sustained competitive advantage?, *Academy of Management Review*, 11, 656–65.

Barney, J.B. (1991) Firm resources and sustained competitive advantage, *Journal of Management*, 17, 99–120.

Bartlett, C.A. and Ghoshal, S. (1989) *Managing across Borders: The Transnational Solution*. London: Century Business.

Baruch, Y. (1988) The rise and fall of organizational commitment, *Human Systems Management*, 17, 135–43.

Bastien, D.T. and Hostager, T.J. (1988) Jazz as a process of organizational innovation, *Communication Research*, 15, 582–602.

Beaumont, P.B. (1992) The US human resource management literature, in G. Salaman *et al.*, (eds) *Human Resource Strategies*. London: Sage.

Becker, B. and Gerhart, B. (1996) The impact of human resource management on organizational performance: progress and prospects, *Academy of Management Review*, 39(4), 779–801.

Bell, D. (1973) *The Coming of the Post-Industrial Society: A Venture in Social Forecasting*. New York, NY: Basic Books.

Berger, P.L. and Luckmann, T. (1967) *The Social Construction of Reality*. Harmondsworth: Penguin.

Black, J.S., Gregersen, H.B. and Mendenhall, M.E. (1992) *Global Assignments: Successfully Expatriating and Repatriating International Managers*. San Francisco, CA: Jossey-Bass.

Blackler, F. (1995) Knowledge, knowledge work and organizations: an overview and interpretation, *Organization Studies*, 16(6), 1021–46.

Blunt P. and Jones, M. (1992) *Managing Organizations in Africa*. Berlin: Walter de Gruyter.

Boisot, M. (1998) *Knowledge Assets: Competitive Advantage in the Information Economy*. Oxford: Oxford University Press.

Bourdieu, P. (1986) The forms of capital, in J.G. Richardson (ed.) *Handbook of Theory and Research for the Sociology of Education*. New York, NY: Greenwood.

Boxall, P.F. (1992) Strategic human resource management: beginnings of a new theoretical sophistication, *Human Resource Management Journal*, 2(3), 60–79.

Boxall, P.F. and Steeneveld, F. (1999) Human resource strategy and competitive advantage: a longitudinal study of engineering consultancies, *Journal of Management Studies*, 36(4), 443–63.

Boyacigiller, N. and Adler, N. (1991) The parochial dinosaur: organizational science in a global context, *Academy of Management Review*, 16(2), 262–90.

References

Brass, D.N. (1995) A social network perspective on HRM, in *Research in Personnel and Human Resources Management*, Vol. 13. Greenwich, CT: JAI Press.

Braverman, H. (1974) *Labour and Monopoly Capitalism*. New York, NY: Monthly Review Press.

Brewster, C. (1999) Strategic human resource management: the value of different paradigms, in R.S. Schuler and S.E Jackson (eds) *Strategic Human Resource Management*. Oxford: Blackwell.

Brewster, C., Tregaskis, O., Hegewisch, A. and Mayne, L. (1996) Comparative research in human resource management: a review and an example, *International Journal of Human Resource Management*, 7, 585–604.

Bryant, C.G. and Jarry, D. (1991) *Giddens' Theory of Structuration: A Critical Appreciation*. London: Routledge.

Budhwar, P. and Debrah, Y.A. (in press) *HRM in Developing Countries*. London: Routledge.

Burack, E.H. (1993) *Corporate Resurgence and the New Employment Relationship*. Westport, CT: Quorum Books.

Cappelli, P. and Singh, H. (1992) Integrating strategic human resources and strategic management, in D. Lewin, O. Mitchell, and P. Scheller (eds) *Research Frontiers in Industrial Relations*. Madison, WI: Industrial Relations Research Association.

Castanias, R.P. and C.E. Helfat (1991) Managerial resources and rents, *Journal of Management*, 17, 155–77.

Chapman, M. (1996) Social anthropology, business studies and cultural issues, *International Studies of Management and Organizations*, 26(4), 3–29.

Child, J. (1987) Information technology, organization and response to strategic challenges, *California Management Review*, 30(1), 33–50.

Clark, P. (2000) *Organizations in Action: Competition between Contexts*. London: Routledge.

Clark, T., Gospel, H. and Montgomery, J. (1999) Running on the spot? A review of twenty years of research on the management of human resources in comparative and international perspective, *International Journal of Human Resource Management*, 10(3), 520–44.

Coase, R. (1937) The nature of the firm, *Economica*, 4, 386–405.

Coff, R. (1997) Human assets and management dilemmas: coping with hazards on the road to resource-based theory, *Academy of Management Review*, 22(2), 374–402.

Coff, R. (1999) When competitive advantage doesn't lead to performance: the resource-based view and stakeholder bargaining power, *Organization Science*, 10(2), 119–33.

Cohen, W.M. and Levinthal, D.A. (1990) Absorptive capacity: a new perspective on learning and innovation, *Administrative Science Quarterly*, 35, 128–52.

Colling, T. (1995) Experiencing turbulence: competition, strategic choice and the management of human resources in British Airways, *Human Resource Management Journal*, 5(5), 18–33.

Cunha, M.P., Cunha, J.V. and Kamoche, K. (1999) Organizational improvisation: what, when, how and why, *International Journal of Management Reviews*, 1, 299–341.

Dandeker, C. (1990) *Surveillance, Power and Modernity*. Cambridge: Polity Press.

Dastmalchian, A., Lee, S. and Ng, I. (2000) The interplay between organizational and national cultures: a comparison of organizational practices in Canada and South Korea using the Competing Values Framework, *International Journal of Human Resource Management*, 11, 388–412.

Davis, K. and Moore, W.E. (1966) Some principles of stratification, in R. Bendix and S.M. Lipset (eds) *Class, Status and Power*. London: Routledge and Kegan Paul.

Day, G.S. and Wensley, R. (1983) Marketing theory with a strategic orientation, *Journal of Marketing*, 47, 78–89.

Deal, T.E. and Kennedy, A.A. (1982) *Corporate Cultures*. Reading, MA: Addison-Wesley.

Debrah, Y.A. and Reid, E.F. (1998) Internet professionals: job skills for an on-line age, *International Journal of Human Resource Management*, 9, 910–33.

Delaney, J.T. and Huselid, M.A. (1996) The impact of human resource management practices on perceptions of organizational performance, *Academy of Management Journal*, 39, 949–69.

Dierickx, I. and Cool, K. (1989) Asset stock accumulation and sustainability of competitive advantage, *Management Science*, 35, 1504–11.

Ding, D.Z., Goodall, K. and Warner, M. (2000) The end of the 'iron rice-bowl': whither Chinese human resource management? *International Journal of Human Resource Management*, 11, 217–36.

Donaldson, L. (1990) The ethereal hand: organizational economics and management theory, *Academy of Management Review*, 15, 369–81.

Dowling, P.J., Welch, D. and Schuler, R.S. (1999) *International Dimensions of Human Resource Management*. Cincinnati, OH: Southwestern.

Drucker, P. (1992) The new society of organizations, *Harvard Business Review*, September–October, 100.

Drucker, P. (1993) *Post-Capitalist Society*. Oxford: Butterworth-Heinemann.

Du Gay, P. and Salaman, G. (1992) The cult[ure] of the customer, *Journal of Management Studies*, 29(5), 615–33.

Earl, M.J. (1989) *Management Strategies for Information Technology*. Hemel Hempstead: Prentice-Hall.

References

Elliot, P. (1972) *The Sociology of the Professions*. London: Macmillan.

Emery, F.E and Trist, E.L. (1960) Socio-technical systems, in C.W. Churchman and M. Verhulst (eds) *Management Science, Models and Techniques*, Vol. 2. London: Pergamon.

Ferris, G.R., Frink, D.D. and Galang, M.C. (1993) Diversity in the workplace: the human resources management challenges, *Human Resource Planning*, 16, 41–51.

Fields, D., Chan, A. and Akhtar, S. (2000) Organizational context and human resource management strategy: a structural equation analysis of Hong Kong firms, *International Journal of Human Resource Management*, 11, 264–77.

Fombrun, C., Tichy, N.M., and Devanna, M.A. (eds) (1984) *Strategic Human Resource Management*. New York, NY: Wiley.

Forster, N. (1994) The forgotten employees? The experiences of expatriate staff returning to the UK, *International Journal of Human Resource Management*, 5(2), 405–25.

Forster, N. (2000) The myth of the 'international manager', *International Journal of Human Resource Management*, 11(1), 126–42.

Foulkes, F.K. (1980) *Personnel Practices in Large Nonunion Companies*. Englewood Cliffs, NJ: Prentice-Hall.

Fukuda, K. and Chu, P. (1994) Wrestling with expatriate family problems: Japanese experience in East Asia, *International Studies of Management and Organization*, 24(3), 36–47.

Fukuyama, F. (1995) *Trust: Social Virtues and the Creation of Prosperity*. London: Hamish Hamilton.

Galang, M.C., Elsik, W. and Russ, G.S. (1999) Legitimacy in human resources management, in *Research in Personnel and Human Resources Management*, Vol. 17. Greenwich, CT: JAI Press.

Galbraith, J. (1967) *The New Industrial State*. Boston, MA: Houghton Mifflin.

Garland, J. and Farmer, R.N. (1986) *International Dimensions of Business Policy and Strategy*. Boston, MA: PWS-Kent.

Giddens, A. (1976) *New Rules for Sociological Method*. London: Hutchinson.

Grant, D. (1999) HRM, rhetoric, and the psychological contract: a case of 'easier said than done', *International Journal of Human Resource Management*, 10, 327–50.

Grant, R.M. (1991a) The resource-based theory of competitive advantage: implications for strategy formulation, *California Management Review*, 33(3), 114–35.

Grant, R.M. (1991b) *Contemporary Strategy Analysis: Concepts, Techniques, Applications*. Cambridge, MA: Basil Blackwell.

Grant, R.M. (1996) Toward a knowledge-based theory of the firm, *Strategic Management Journal*, 17, 109–22.

Guest, D.E. (1987) Human resource management and industrial relations, *Journal of Management Studies*, 24, 503–21.

Guest, D.E. (1989) Human resource management: its implications for industrial relations and trade unions, in J. Storey (ed.) *New Perspectives on Human Resource Management*. London: Routledge.

Guest, D.E. (1990) Human resource management and the American dream, *Journal of Management Studies*, 27(4), 377–97.

Guest, D.E. (1997) Human resource management and performance: a review and research agenda, *International Journal of Human Resource Management*, 8, 263–77.

Gunnigle, P. and Moore, S. (1994) Linking business strategy and human resources management, *Personnel Review*, 23(1), 63–84.

Habermas, J. (1972) *Knowledge and Human Interests*. London: Heinemann.

Hall, R. (1993) A framework linking intangible resources and capabilities to sustainable competitive advantage, *Strategic Management Journal*, 14, 607–18.

Hampden-Turner, C. and Trompenaars, F. (1997) *Mastering the Infinite Game: How Asian Values are Transforming Business Practices*. Oxford: Capstone.

Harvey, M.G. (1982) The other side of foreign assignments: dealing with the repatriation dilemma, *Columbia Journal of World Business*, 17(1), 52–9.

Hatch, M.J. (1999) Exploring the empty spaces of organizing: how improvisational jazz helps redescribe organizational structure, *Organization Studies*, 20, 75–100.

Hayes, R.H. and Wheelwright, S.L. (1984) *Restoring our Competitive Edge: Competing Through Manufacturing*. New York, NY: John Wiley.

Hedlund G. (1981) Autonomy of subsidiaries and formalization of head-quarter–subsidiary relations in Swedish MNCs, in L. Otterbeck (ed.) *The Management of Headquarter–Subsidiary Relations in Multinational Companies*. New York, NY: St Martin's Press.

Hendry, C. (1994) *Human Resource Strategies for International Growth*. London: Routledge.

Hendry, C. and Pettigrew, A. (1986) The practice of strategic human resource management, *Personnel Review*, 15(3), 3–8.

Hendry, C. and Pettigrew, A. (1990) Human resource management: an agenda for the 1990s, *International Journal of Human Resource Management*, 1(1), 17–43.

Heneman III, H.G., Heneman, R.L. and Judge, T.A. (2000) *Staffing Organizations*. Boston, MA: McGraw-Hill.

Hersey, P. and Blanchard, K.H. (1988) *Management and Organizational Behaviour: Utilizing Human Resources*. Englewood Cliffs, NJ: Prentice-Hall.

Hiltrop, J.M. (1995) The changing psychological contract, *European Management Journal*, 13(3), 286–94.

References

Hofstede, G. and Bond, M.H. (1988) The Confucious connection: from cultural roots to economic growth, *Organizational Dynamics*, Spring, 5–21.

Huselid, M.A. (1995) The impact of human resource management practices on turnover, productivity, and corporate financial performance, *Academy of Management Journal*, 38, 635–72.

Huselid, M.A., Jackson, S.E. and Schuler, R.S. (1997) Technical and strategic human resource management effectiveness as determinants of firm performance, *Academy of Management Journal*, 40(1), 171–88.

Ibarra, H. (1992) Homophily and differential return: sex difference in network structure and access in an advertising firm, *Administrative Science Quarterly*, 37, 422–47.

Jackson, S.E. (1992) *Diversity in the Workplace*. New York, NY: Guilford Press.

Jaeger, A.M. and Kanungo, R.N. (1990) (eds) *Management in Developing Countries*. London: Routledge.

Jain, H.C., Lawler, J.J. and Morishima, M. (1998) Multinational corporations, human resource management and host-country nationals, *International Journal of Human Resource Management*, 9, 553–655.

Jensen, M. and Meckling, W. (1976) Theory of the firm: managerial behaviour, agency costs, and ownership structure, *Journal of Financial Economics*, 3, 305–60.

Kamoche, K. (1996a) Strategic human resource management within a resource-capability view of the firm, *Journal of Management Studies*, 33(2), 213–33.

Kamoche, K. (1996b) From human resources to resourcefulness: an agenda for the 21st century, in I. Beardwell (ed.) *Contemporary Developments in Human Resource Management*. Paris: Editions ESKA.

Kamoche, K. (1996c) The integration–differentiation puzzle: a resource-capability perspective in international human resource management, *International Journal of Human Resource Management*, 7, 230–44.

Kamoche, K. (2000a) *Sociological Paradigms and Human Resources: An African Context*. Aldershot: Ashgate.

Kamoche, K. (2000b) From boom to bust: the challenges of managing people in Thailand, *International Journal of Human Resource Management*, 11(2), 452–68.

Kamoche, K. and Cunha, M.P. (1999) Teamwork, knowledge-creation and improvisation, in M.P. Cunha and C.A. Marques (eds) *Readings in Organization Science*. Lisbon: ISPA.

Kamoche, K. and Mueller, F. (1998) Human resource management and the appropriation–learning perspective, *Human Relations*, 51(8), 1033–60.

Kanter, R.M. (1990) *When Giants Learn to Dance*. New York, NY: Simon & Schuster.

Kay, J. (1995) *Foundations of Corporate Success: How Business Strategies add Value*. Oxford: Oxford University Press.

Keenoy, T. (1990) HRM: a case of the wolf in sheep's clothing, *Personnel Review*, 19(2), 3–9.

Kiggundu, M.N. (1989) *Managing Organizations in Developing Countries*. West Hartford, CT: Kumarian Press.

Kilmann, R.H., Saxton, M.J., Serpa, R. and Associates (1985) *Gaining Control of the Corporate Culture*. San Francisco, CA: Jossey-Bass.

Kim, J.K. and Nam, S.H. (1998) The concept and dynamics of face: implications for organizational behaviour in Asia, *Organization Science*, 9, 522–34.

Knights, D.F., Murray, F. and Wilmott, H. (1993) Networking as knowledge work: a study of interorganizational development in the financial services sector, *Journal of Management Studies*, 30: 975–96.

Kobrin, S.J. (1988) Expatriate reduction and strategic control in American multinational corporations, *Human Resource Management*, 27, 63–75.

Kochan, T.A., Batt, R. and Dyer, L. (1992) International human resource studies: a framework for future research, in D. Lewin, O. Mitchell, and P. Scheller (eds) *Research Frontiers in Industrial Relations*. Madison, WI: Industrial Relations Research Association.

Kochan, T.A., Katz, H.C. and McKersie, R.B. (1986) *The Transformation of American Industrial Relations*. New York, NY: Basic Books.

Kogut, B. (1991) Country capabilities and the permeability of borders, *Strategic Management Journal*, 12(3), 33–47.

Kogut, B. and Zander, U. (1992) Knowledge of the firm, combinative capabilities and the replication of technology, *Organization Science*, 3, 383–97.

Kogut, B. and Zander, U. (1996) What do firms do? Coordination, identity and learning, *Organization Science*, 7, 502–18.

Kotter, J.P. and Schlesinger, L.A. (1979) Choosing strategies for change, *Harvard Business Review*, March–April, 106–14.

Kuhn, T.S. (1962) *The Structure of Scientific Revolutions*. Chicago, IL: University of Chicago Press.

Kunda, G. (1992) *Engineering Culture*. Philadelphia, PA: Temple University Press.

Lawler III, E.E. (1984) Performance appraisal practices of reward systems, in C. Fombrun, N.M. Tichy and M.A. Devanna (eds) *Strategic Human Resource Management*. New York, NY: Wiley.

Legge, K. (1989) Human resource management: a critical analysis, in J. Storey (ed.) *New Perspectives on Human Resource Management*. London: Routledge.

Legge, K. (1995) *Human Resource Management: Rhetorics and Realities*. Houndsmills: Macmillan.

References

Legge, K. (1997) The morality of HRM, in C. Mabey, D. Skinner, and T.A.R. Clark (eds) *Experiencing Human Resource Management*. London: Sage.

Lengnick-Hall, C.A. and Lengnick-Hall, M.L. (1988) Strategic human resource management: a review of the literature and a proposed typology, *Academy of Management Review*, 13, 454–70.

Leung, K., Smith, P.B. and Wang, Z. (1996) Job satisfaction in joint venture hotels in China: an organizational justice analysis, *Journal of International Business Studies*, 27, 947–62.

Lippman, S. and Rumelt, R. (1982) Uncertain imitability: an analysis of interfirm differences in efficiency under competition, *Bell Journal of Economics*, 13, 418–38.

Liu, M., Denis, H., Kolodny, H. and Stymme, B. (1990) Organization design for technological change, *Human Relations*, 43(1), 7–22.

Lowenstein, R. (1997) Microsoft and its two constituencies, *Wall Street Journal*, 4 Dec, p. C1.

Mabey, C. and Salaman, G. (1995) *Strategic Human Resource Management*. Oxford: Blackwell.

Mabey, C., Salaman, G. and Storey, J. (1998) *Human Resource Management: A Strategic Introduction*. Oxford: Blackwell.

Mahoney, J.T. and Pandian, J.R. (1992) The resource-based view within the conversation of strategic management, *Strategic Management Journal*, 13, 363–80.

Mamman, A. and Richards, D. (1996) Perceptions and possibilities of intercultural adjustment: some neglected characteristics of expatriates, *International Business Review*, 5(3), 283–301.

Marschan-Piekkari, R., Welch, D.E. and Welch, L.S. (1999) Adopting a common corporate language: IHRM implications, *International Journal of Human Resource Management*, 10, 377–90.

Martin, R. (1977) *The Sociology of Knowledge*. London: Routledge and Kegan Paul.

Masterman, M. (1970) The nature of a paradigm, in I. Lakatos and A. Musgrave (eds) *Criticisms and the Growth of Knowledge*. Cambridge, MA: Cambridge University Press.

Meakin, D. (1976) *Man and Work: Literature and Culture in Industrial Society*. London: Methuen.

Mendenhall, M., Dunbar, E. and Oddou, G. (1987) Expatriate selection, training and career-pathing, *Human Resource Management*, 26, 331–45.

Miles, R. and Snow, C. (1984) Designing strategic human resource systems, *Organizational Dynamics*, Summer, 36–53.

Milgrom, P. and Roberts, J. (1992) *Economics, Organization and Management*. Englewood Cliffs, NJ: Prentice-Hall.

Miller, P. (1996) Strategy and the ethical management of human resources, *Human Resource Management Journal*, 6(1), 5–18.

Milliman, J., Von Glinow, M.A. and Nathan, M. (1991) Organizational life cycles and strategic international human resource management in multinational companies: implications for congruence theory, *Academy of Management Review*, 16, 318–39.

Mintzberg, H. (1983) *Power In and Around Organizations*. Englewood Cliffs, NJ: Prentice-Hall.

Morris, J. and Steers, R. (1980) Structural influences on organizational commitment, *Journal of Vocational Behaviour*, 17, 50–7.

Morrison, W.E. and Robinson, S. (1997) When employees feel betrayed: a model of how psychological contract violation develops, *Academy of Management Review*, 22, 301–26.

Mowday, R.T. (1998) Reflections of the study and relevance of organizational commitment, *Human Resource Management Review*, 8, 387–401.

Mueller, F. (1996) Human resources as strategic assets: an evolutionary resource-based theory, *Journal of Management Studies*, 33, 757–85.

Nahapiet, J. and Ghoshal, S. (1998) Social capital, intellectual capital, and the organizational advantage, *Academy of Management Review*, 23(2), 242–66.

Napier, N.K. and Vu, V.T. (1998) International human resource management in developing and transitional economy countries: a breed apart?, *Human Resource Management Review*, 8(1), 39–77.

Nelson, R.R. and Winter, S.G. (1982) *An Evolutionary Theory of Economic Change*. Cambridge, MA: Belknap Press.

Nonaka, I. (1994) A dynamic theory of organizational knowledge creation, *Organization Science*, 5(1), 14–37.

Nonaka, I. and Takeuchi, H. (1995) *The Knowledge Creating Company*. New York, NY: Oxford University Press.

Ogbonna, E. (1992) Organization culture and human resource management: dilemmas and contradictions, in P. Blyton and P. Turnbull (eds) *Reassessing Human Resource Management*. London: Sage.

Ohmae, K. (1989) The global logic of strategic alliances, *Harvard Business Review*, March/April, 143–55.

Olmstead, V.H. (1900) The betterment of industrial conditions, *Bulletin of the Department of Labour*, 31, 1117–56. Washington, DC: Government Printing Office.

Onyemelukwe, C.C. (1973) *Men and Management in Contemporary Africa*. London: Longman.

Ouchi, W.G. (1981) *Theory Z*. Reading, MA: Addison-Wesley.

Owen, R. (1813) *A New View of Society, or Essays on the Principle of the Formation of the Human Character and the Application of the Principle to Practice*. London: Richard Taylor.

Pedler, M., Burgoyne, J. and Boydell, T. (1991) *The Learning Company*. London: McGraw-Hill.

References

Penrose, E.T. (1959) *The Theory of the Growth of the Firm.* Oxford: Blackwell.

Peters, T.J. and Waterman Jr, R.H. (1982) *In Search of Excellence: Lessons from America's Best-Run Companies.* New York, NY: Harper & Row.

Pfeffer, J. (1992) Understanding power in organizations, *California Management Review*, Winter, 29–50.

Pfeffer, J. (1998) *The Human Equation.* Cambridge, MA: Harvard Business School Press.

Pfeffer, J. and Salancik, G.R. (1978) *The External Control of Organizations: A Resource Dependence Perspective.* New York, NY: Harper & Row.

Polanyi, M. (1962) *Personal Knowledge: Towards a Post-Critical Philosophy.* London: Routledge and Kegan Paul.

Polanyi, M. (1967) *The Tacit Dimension.* London: Routledge and Kegan Paul.

Poole, M. (1990) Editorial: human resource management in an international perspective, *International Journal of Human Resource Management*, 1, 1–15.

Poole, M. (ed.) (1999) *Human Resource Management: Critical Perspectives on Business and Management.* London: Routledge.

Poole, M. and Jenkins, G. (1990) *The Impact of Economic Democracy: Profit-Sharing and Employee-Shareholding.* London: Routledge.

Porter, M.E. (1980) *Competitive Advantage: Creating and Sustaining Superior Performance.* New York, NY: Free Press.

Porter, M.E. and Millar, V. (1985) How information gives you competitive advantage, *Harvard Business Review*, July–August, 63, 149–61.

Purcell, J. (1989) The impact of corporate strategy on HRM, in J. Storey (ed.) *New Perspectives on Human Resource Management.* London: Routledge and Kegan Paul.

Purcell, J. and Ahlstrand, B. (1989) Corporate strategies and the management of employee relations in the multidivisional company, *British Journal of Industrial Relations*, November, 396–417.

Purcell, J. and Ahlstrand, B. (1994) *Human Resource Management in the Multidivisional Company.* Oxford: Oxford University Press.

Pym, D. (1979) Work is good, employment is bad, *Employee Relations*, 1(1), 16–18.

Redding, S.G. (1990) *The Spirit of Chinese Capitalism.* New York, NY: Walter de Gruyter.

Reed, M. (1992) *The Sociology of Organizations: Themes, Perspectives and Prospects.* London: Harvester Wheatsheaf.

Reed, R. and DeFillippi, R.J. (1990) Causal ambiguity, barriers to imitation and sustained competitive advantage, *Academy of Management Review*, 15, 88–102.

Robinson, S.L. and Rousseau, D.M. (1994) Violating the psychological contract: not the exception but the norm, *Journal of Organizational Behaviour*, 15, 245–59.

Robinson, S.L., Kraatz, M.S. and Rousseau, D.M. (1994) Changing obligations and the psychological contract: a longitudinal study, *Academy of Management Journal*, 37, 137–52.

Rosen, S. and Juris, H. (1995) Ethical issues in human resource management, in G. Ferris, S. Rosen and D. Barnum (eds) *Handbook of Human Resource Management*. Cambridge, MA: Blackwell.

Rosenzweig, P.M. and Singh, J.V. (1991) Organizational environments and the multinational enterprise, *Academy of Management Review*, 16, 340–61.

Rousseau, D.M. (1995) *Psychological Contracts in Organizations: Understanding Written and Unwritten Agreements*. London: Sage.

Rumelt, R.P. (1984) Towards a theory of the firm, in R.B. Lamb (ed.) *Competitive Strategic Management*. Englewood Cliffs, NJ: Prentice-Hall.

Russell, J.S., Terborg, J.R., and Powers, M.L. (1985) Organizational performance and organizational level training and support, *Personnel Psychology*, 38, 849–63.

Schein, E.H. (1978) *Career Dynamics: Matching Individuals and Organizational Needs*. Reading, MA: Addison-Wesley.

Schuler, R.S. (1989) Strategic human resource management and industrial relations, *Human Relations*, 42(2), 57–84.

Schuler, R.S. (forthcoming) The internationalization of human resource management, *Journal of International Management*.

Schuler, R.S. and Jackson, S.E. (1987) Organizational strategy and organizational level as determinants of HRM Processes, *Human Resource Planning*, 10(3): 121–41.

Schuler, R.S. and Jackson, S.E. (1999) (eds) *Strategic Human Resource Management*. Oxford: Blackwell.

Scullion, H. (1993) Creating international managers: recruitment and development issues, in P. Kirkbride (ed.) *Human Resource Management in Europe*. London: Routledge.

Scullion, H. (1995) International human resource management, in J. Storey (ed) *Human Resource Management: A Critical Text*. London: Routledge.

Schumpeter, J. ([1911] 1968) *The Theory of Economic Development*. Cambridge, MA: Harvard University Press.

Selmer, J. (1999) Adjustment to Hong Kong: US and European expatriates, *Human Resource Management Journal*, 9(3), 83–93.

Senge, P.M. (1990) *The Fifth Discipline: The Age and Practice of the Learning Organization*. London: Century Business.

Siebert, W.S. and Addison, J.T. (1991) Internal labour markets: causes and consequences, *Oxford Review of Economic Policy*, 7(1), 76–92.

Siehl, L. and Smith, D. (1990) Avoiding the loss of a gain: retaining top managers in an acquisition, *Human Resource Management*, 29, 167–85.

Sisson, K. (1989) Personnel management in transition, in K. Sisson (ed.) *Personnel Management in Britain*, Oxford: Blackwell.

References

Sisson, K. and Sullivan, T. (1987) Editorial: Management strategy and industrial relations, *Journal of Management Studies*, 24(5), 427–32.

Skinner, W. (1981) Big hat, no cattle: managing human resources, *Harvard Business Review*, 47(3), 136–45.

Snell, R. (1999) Managing ethically, in L. Fulop and S. Linstead (eds) *Management: A Critical Text*. South Yarra, Australia: Macmillan.

Sparrow, P.R. (1998) Is HRM in crisis?, in P.R. Sparrow and M. Marchington (eds) *Human Resource Management: The New Agenda*. London: Financial Times/Pitman.

Spender, J.-C. (1996) Making knowledge the basis of a dynamic theory of the firm, *Strategic Management Journal*, 17(S2), 45–62.

Stalk Jr, G. (1988) Time – the next source of competitive advantage, *Harvard Business Review*, 66(4), 41–51.

Starbuck, W. (1992) Learning by knowledge intensive firms, *Journal of Management Studies*, 29, 713–40.

Storey, J. (ed.) (1989) *New Perspectives on Human Resource Management*. London: Routledge.

Storey, J. (1992) *Developments in the Management of Human Resources*. Oxford: Blackwell.

Suchman, M.C. (1995) Managing legitimacy: strategic and institutional approaches, *Academy of Management Review*, 20, 571–610.

Teece, D.J. (1982) Towards an economic theory of the multiproduct firm, *Journal of Economic Behaviour and Organization*, 3, 39–63.

Teece, D.J. (1986) Firm boundaries, technological innovation and strategic management, in L.G. Thomas III (ed.) *The Economics of Strategic Planning*. Lexington, MA: D.C. Heath.

Terpstra, D.E. and Rozell, E.J. (1993) The relationship of staffing practices to organizational level measures of performance, *Personnel Psychology*, 46, 27–48.

Tichy, N.M., Fombrun, C.J. and Devanna, M.A. (1982) Strategic human resource management, *Sloan Management Review*, Winter, 47–61.

Tolman, W.H. (1900) *Industrial Betterment*. New York, NY: Social Services Press.

Toyoda, E. (1987) *Toyota: Fifty Years in Motion*. Tokyo: Kodansha International.

Tripsas, M. (1997) Unravelling the process of creative destruction: complementary assets and incumbent survival in the typesetter industry, *Strategic Management Journal*, 18, 119–42.

Tsang, D. (1999) Customs fight back over piracy claims, *South China Morning Post*, 5 November.

Tsui, A. and Fahr, L. (1997) When *guanxi* matters: relational demography and *guanxi* in the Chinese context, *Work and Occupations*, 24, 56–79.

Tung, R.L. (1987) Expatriate assignments: enhancing success and minimising failure, *Academy of Management Executive*, 1, 117–26.

Tung, R.L. (1996) Managing in Asia: cross-cultural dimensions, in P. Joynt and M. Warner (eds) *Managing across Cultures: Issues and Perspectives.* London: International Thompson Business Press.

Tung, R.L. (1998) American expatriates abroad: from neophytes to cosmopolitans, *Journal of World Business*, 33, 125–44.

Tyson, S. (1995) *Human Resource Strategy.* London: Pitman.

Ulrich, D. (1997) Measuring Human Resources, *Human Resource Management*, 36(3), 303–20.

Van Maanen, J. and Schein, E.H. (1979) Toward a theory of organizational socialization, in B.M. Staw (ed.) *Research in Organizational Behaviour*, Vol. 1. Greenwich, CT: JAI Press.

Warner, M. (1995) *The Management of Human Resources in Chinese Industry.* London: Macmillan.

Watson, T.J. (1986) *Management, Organization and Employment Strategy: New Directions in Theory and Practice.* London: Routledge and Kegan Paul.

Watson, T.J. (1989) *Sociology, Work and Industry.* London: Routledge.

Weick, K.E. (1998) Improvisation as a mindset for organizational analysis, *Organization Science*, 9, 543–55.

Welbourne, T.M. and Andrews, A.O. (1996) Predicting performance of initial public offerings: should human resource management be in the equation? *Academy of Management Journal*, 11(2), 801–14.

Welch, D.E. and Welch, L.S. (1997) Pre-expatriation: the role of HR factors in the early stages of internationalization, *International Journal of Human Resource Management*, 8, 402–13.

Wernerfelt, B. (1984) A resource-based view of the firm, *Strategic Management Journal*, 5, 171–80.

Whitley, R. (1992) *Business Systems in East Asia: Firms, Markets and Societies.* London: Sage.

Williamson, O.E. (1975) *Markets and Hierarchies Analysis and Antitrust Implications: A Study in the Economics of Internal Organization.* New York, NY: Free Press.

Williamson, O.E. (1987) The economics of organization: the transaction cost approach, *American Journal of Sociology*, 87, 548–77.

Wright, P.M., McMahan, G.C. and McWilliams, A. (1994) Human resources and sustained competitive advantage: a resource-based perspective, *International Journal of Human Resource Management*, 5, 301–26.

Wright, P.M., Smart, D.L. and McMahan, G.C. (1995) Matches between human resources and strategy among NCAA basketball teams, *Academy of Management Journal*, 38(4), 1052–74.

Wright, P.M. and Snell, A.S. (1998) Toward a unifying framework for exploring fit and flexibility in strategic human resource management, *Academy of Management Journal*, 23, 756–72.

INDEX

Index

Index

Index

surveillance systems, 65, 76, 86
switching costs, 68, 69, 73
symbolic interaction, 87

tacit knowledge, 9, 46, 65, 78, 80, 85,
    89–90, 107, 113, 119, 122–4
Takeuchi, H., 76, 78, 90, 122
talent, 46, 49, 54, 64, 6
Taylor, Frederick, 13
Taylorism, 13–14
teamwork, 15, 85, 89
technocracy, 75
technological revolution, 14–15
technology, 3, 16
    automation, 19, 75
    knowledge management, 15, 75–6,
        78, 84–6, 88
    socio-technical system, 14
    transfer, 20
Teece, D.J., 45, 46, 71, 72
telecommunications, 14
Terpstra, D.E., 52
Tichy, N.M., 28, 29
time compression diseconomies, 47,
    53, 83
time management, 65
Tolman, W.H., 12
total quality management, 19
Toyoda, E., 72
Toyota, 72
trade unions, 16, 24–5, 66–7
training, 8, 16, 17, 36–9, 46, 67, 69, 94,
    98
transaction cost economics, 68, 72–3,
    89
transfer pricing, 105
transitional economies, 101–2, 105
transnational firms, 97
Tripsas, M., 72
Trist, E.L., 14
Trompenaars, F., 24
trust, 48, 49, 62, 86
Tsang, D., 71
Tsui, A., 102
Tung, R.L., 68, 94, 102
Tyson, S., 30, 118

Ulrich, D., 31, 52

unitarism, 15, 24–5, 60, 74, 78–9, 81,
    117, 120
United Nations Conference on Trade
    and Development (UNCTAD),
    109
universalist paradigm, 32
university courses, 39–40
utilitarianism, 116

value
    added, *see* added value
    chain, 44
    of employees, 6, 28, 30, 40–2
    of human resources, 27, 34–40
Van Maanen, J., 113
virtual organizations, 116
Vu, V.T., 41, 101, 102

wages, 60, 82, 99, 105
Wall Street Journal, 70
Warner, M., 102
Waterman, R.H., 22, 36–7
Watson, T.J., 15, 83
Weick, K.E., 122
Welbourne, T.M., 33
Welch, D.E., 98
Welch, L.S., 98
welfare improvement programme,
    12–14
welfare officers, 13
welfare state, 18
weltanschauung, 81
Wensley, R., 27
Wernerfelt, B., 45
Wheelwright, S.L., 27
Whitley, R., 24
Williamson, O.E., 72–3
Winter, S.G., 45, 120
World Bank, 109
World Economic Forum (Davos), 109
World Trade Organization, 109
Wright, P.M., 29, 32, 46, 54

Young Men's Christian Association, 13

Zander, U., 89, 112, 121
zero defects, 23
zones of manoeuvre, 70, 73